The Power Of Intentional Leadership

How You Can Transform Your Team To Produce Extraordinary Results

Ted Easton

© Copyright 2021 - All rights reserved.

It is not legal to reproduce, duplicate, or transmit any part of this document in either electronic means or in printed format. Recording of this publication is strictly prohibited and any storage of this document is not allowed unless with written permission from the publisher except for the use of brief quotations in a book review.

Table of Contents

Introduction

Chapter One: Developing The Leader's Mindset

Chapter Two: Say:Do Ratio

Chapter Three: Communicating Success

Chapter Four: Consistent Feedback Culture

Chapter Five: Praise & Criticism - When & Where

Chapter Six: Leading Through Change

Chapter Seven: The Art Of Duck Leadership

Chapter Eight: Patience, Flexibility, & Adaptability

Chapter Nine: Filling Your Self-Development Bucket

Conclusion

Introduction

The Precipitating Effects of Poor Leadership

Poor leadership skills lead to several problems with the employees and the organization. Ineffective leadership is the root cause of communication issues, low morale of employees, constant conflict, a lack of responsibility and initiative, and considerable resistance to change. Poor leaders are indecisive and often hurt the organization's bottom line. They are seldom able to engage their employees, which affects their performance adversely.

Bad leaders often fail to provide feedback that can make a difference to the employee, and eventually to the organization. They are ineffective with both praise and criticism, and employees are either left guessing or hurt when they are reprimanded in a disrespectful way. In many cases, leaders are responsible for the high rates of attrition, absenteeism, and low morale. Bad leaders often cannot set priorities and lack focus and inspiration. Their own lack of direction prevents them from giving any meaningful direction to their employees. Bad leaders have teams that are often unproductive, which leads to a lack of growth in the organization.

Bad leadership is quite noticeable to the onlooker. If you are a leader, these traits can help you understand what hurts the employees and the organization, and make corrections to your own leadership style. Bad leaders are seldom popular among their team, and more than one team member complains about their style. You will often notice multiple complaints about the leader, clients, and members of other departments. Sometimes, leaders have poor or no listening skills and fail to acknowledge the opinion of their team members, giving rise to more problems. Furthermore, micromanagement is a definite sign of bad leadership and leads to resentment among employees. A lack of autonomy breeds insecurity among employees and leads to adverse outcomes.

The Power Of Intentional Leadership

Learn the Profound Impact of Effective Leadership

"The Power of Intentional Leadership" is a very different way to describe true leadership. While you may understand there are several elements to successful leadership such as communication, feedback, adaptability, and change management, the way these elements interact depends on the caliber of the leader. Knowing how to put them into practice affects your outcomes in a profound manner.

The first thing a leader needs to understand is the ability to have the right mindset. There are many subtle ways your mindset can influence your beliefs, and therefore, your actions. Fixed or implemental mindsets, for example, are quite rigid and adversely affect your leadership role. Having a mindset that encourages growth, learning, and more is the key to leadership success. Another important trait of good leadership is to practice what is preached, that is to close the gap between "say" and "do", and follow through promises made to the team and customers. Leaders must be able to communicate well. Good and clear communication is the cornerstone of trust in an organization. Conversely, poor communication leaves the team demotivated, frustrated, and unhappy. Leaders need strategies such as asking questions with empathy, knowing when to talk and when to listen, and maintaining open body language.

The next thing that spells the value of leadership is feedback and the ability to praise and criticize effectively. A positive and consistent feedback culture is great for any company, and immediate feedback is the way to bring about a positive change. Besides, leaders must make it a point to praise more and criticize less, and praise intentionally to achieve the best employee performance. Change management is a critical aspect of leadership success, and specific strategies such as planning, sharing information, addressing questions, and managing conflict make it a successful process.

Change management requires empathy and the ability of a leader to manage the expectations of the team. Finally, leaders can apply specific styles of leadership, such as duck leadership to achieve success with leading teams and giving the best performance even in adversity. Transformational leadership is always accompanied by flexibility, patience, and adaptability, and the importance of these three key qualities can never be understated. Even when leaders possess the best traits, self-development is the best strategy for the growth of the leader and his team.

If you want to be an effective leader, this is absolutely the right place to get into an absorbing journey with David and Goliath. As you observe David through the chapters, he shows exactly what to do to become someone your team will look up to for guidance, how to make a real difference to someone who works with you, and how to make waves in the strategic positioning of your organization.

With detailed explanations accompanying the story of David, Goliath, and their teams, you will be able to answer the questions that lingered in your mind all this while. As you read through the book, you will understand several aspects that matter to a leader, from the most subtle to the most pronounced facets. "The Power of Intentional Leadership" serves as a comprehensive guide to the best practices of effective leadership. It tells you a story you will not forget!

Chapter One: Developing The Leader's Mindset

Here's a little story of David, a leader with a "growth" mindset, and Goliath, a leader with a "fixed mindset". Both leaders face a similar challenge where they are expected to communicate the organization's future direction to board members. They approach the problem very differently and have strikingly different outcomes. Here's what happens…

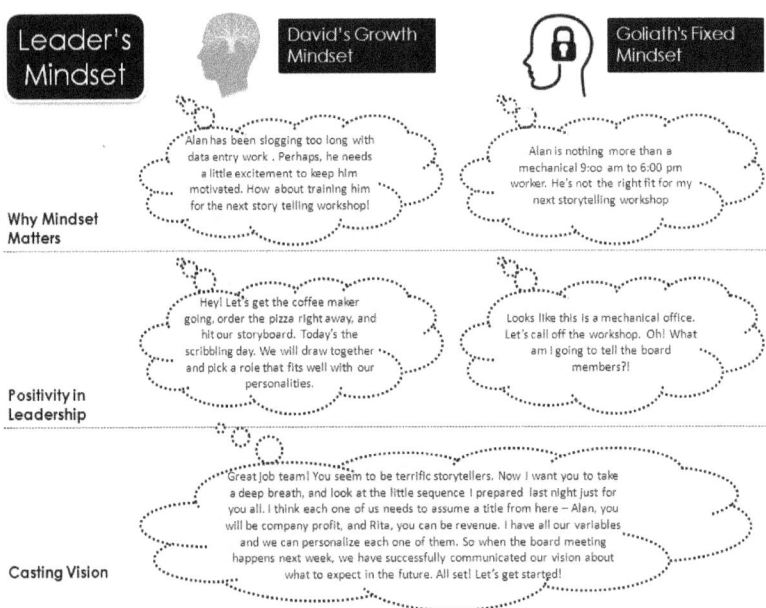

If you have been wondering what could be the single element with the potential to influence your leadership moves inside-out, then you are in the right place.

An immensely impactful aspect of successful leadership that flows into the attitude and behavior of leaders is the leadership mindset. What happens in your head tells a lot about how your leadership story will unfold.

What's So Bad About the Wrong Leadership Mindset

To be good at developing the right mindset, it is important to first understand what could go wrong. Here are five wrong mindsets you want to understand to make sure you step away from areas that may hurt you during your leadership experiences (*To Be a Great Leader, You Need the Right Mindset*, 2020):

Fixed Mindset

If you are trying to lead with a fixed mindset, you probably think that individuals do not change - you probably assume that it is never possible for the members of your team to change their gifts, capacities, and insight (*To Be a Great Leader, You Need the Right Mindset*, 2020). If you have this mindset, you are likely to believe that failure has a deep impact and you may consider yourself a failure. That makes you more prone to giving up.

Performance Mindset

If you have a performance mindset, you are probably motivated to get favorable judgments about your competence (*To Be a Great Leader, You Need the Right Mindset*, 2020). If you feel you tend to avoid negative judgments, then you may find yourself less open to learning and receiving honest feedback about your competence. As a result, you may become less cooperative and adaptable.

Implemental Mindsets

Having an implemental mindset makes you shift your focus towards only making decisions. You may not be receptive to information or new ideas (*To Be a Great Leader, You Need the Right Mindset*, 2020). This attitude may make you a bad decision-maker. An implemental mindset also makes leaders less open to feedback.

Prevention Mindset

A prevention mindset is one that induces thinking that leads to avoiding losses and problems. If you have inadvertently developed this mindset, then the bad news is that you are closed to change and setbacks and challenges may prompt negative thoughts (*To Be a Great Leader, You Need the Right Mindset*, 2020). This mindset is likely to adversely affect innovation and performance.

Inward Mindset

If you have a tendency of seeing people as objects, then agree or not, a drastic change in thinking is highly desirable at this point (*To Be a Great Leader, You Need the Right Mindset*, 2020). You probably got into this thinking if you perceived yourself as more important than others. The sad part about this type of thinking is the insensitivity that is most likely to develop with regard to the emotions and feelings of followers. Leaders with an inward mindset are seldom able to look at their faults, and end up accusing others when something turns out bad.

Independent Mindset

If you are leading a team with an independent mindset, then you may end up worrying about your own prosperity (Byrd, 2020). You may not feel the need to consult your team before taking on a new challenge. If you have information but do not share that with your team, then it becomes an uphill task to build trust among team members. In most situations that are primed for the joint effort of a team, an individualistic approach may make the team less resilient.

That's about most of the aspects that probably go into making a leadership development initiative ineffective. As the BrandonHall Group put it, 329 organizations in their 2013 survey jointly indicated that 75% of their programs were ineffective (*To Be a Great Leader, You Need the Right Mindset*, 2020). Their research also pointed out that the thing that is lacking in most leadership development programs is the mindset of leaders or "how leaders think, learn, and behave".

Why the Right Mindset Could Be the Key to your Leadership Success

On the contrary, engaging in an appropriate mindset influences the attitude of leaders and their behavior. Eventually, it affects their long-term attitude. Leadership is influenced by thoughts, which have an impact on actions. Actions influence results which eventually form the basis of beliefs (Clark, 2020). Understanding mindsets helps identify actions required for effective results. If you want to be a successful leader, the right mindset is an absolute necessity. Here is a list of recommended mindsets that may contribute to your leadership success:

Growth Mindset

A growth mindset helps talents and capabilities flourish, encourages the act of seeking knowledge, and is good for change. Research has found that if you have a growth mindset, then you are ready for challenges, don't mind feedback, and are a great problem-solver (To Be a Great Leader, You Need the Right Mindset, 2020). Your positive growth approach drives you towards providing developmental feedback to team members. The best part is that you are a persistent goal seeker and are able to hit your goals most of the time.

Learning Mindset

A learning attitude sets you up for a constant pursuit towards learning and expanding your competence (To Be a Great Leader, You Need the Right Mindset, 2020). You are highly motivated to learn and try different strategies to get to the core of the subject area.

You strive hard and are receptive to feedback. You are ready to adapt and are persistent in learning. If you are primed for the learning mindset, then most people will find you cooperative and a high performer.

Promotion Mindset

Having a promotion mindset means that winning and gains matter most to you. They are focused at seeking a specific goal or purpose and pursue it fervently (To Be a Great Leader, You Need the Right Mindset, 2020). A promotional mindset promotes positive thinking, persistence in the face of challenges, and openness to change. Moreover, the attitude makes you innovative and a high performer.

Deliberative Mindset

Leaders with a deliberative mindset have increased responsiveness to a wide variety of information as the basis of their optimal performance (To Be a Great Leader, You Need the Right Mindset, 2020). If you are a leader with a deliberative mindset, then you are a better decision-maker. Your mindset is one that promotes an impartial outlook, reduces bias, and promotes a greater level of accuracy.

Outward Mindset

An outward mindset is the best thing that can happen to you. You value the people around you and feel that it is important to have them (Gottfredson, 2018). Your outward mindset helps you introspect about what went wrong when there is a problem.

Interdependent Mindset

The word 'team' suggests joint effort, which is the essence of the interdependent mindset. When you are able to foster an interdependent attitude between team members, you become an enabler to shift the thinking from being egoistic to contributing towards the broader vision of the company (Byrd, 2020). Thinking about the team's goals as opposed to individual goals drives team members towards feeling responsible about the whole team and also providing support to the whole team. The interdependent mindset is the truly collaborative mindset. It is the mindset that makes a cohesive team and provides a sense of security. This, in turn, promotes a risk-taking attitude due to the support guarantee from fellow members of the team. Team members do not feel threatened by the success of their peers, and working together is quite enjoyable.

Curious Mindset

Your curious mindset encourages you to find learning lessons in your failures. A curious mindset promotes the creative person in you and you are less likely to be defensive. On the contrary, you are looking single-mindedly at solutions that work. Curiosity becomes the crux of your problem-solving approach, and your team is far from the tendency to blame others (Byrd, 2020). Your questions are not judgemental, for they ask what went wrong and what were the factors responsible for it. Leaders with a curious mindset are focused on finding better approaches to arrive at better outcomes in the future. They try to deeply understand failures and the opportunities it has for their future success. Curiosity helps them get to the root of the problem and not blaming others translates to psychological safety.

Long-Term Mindset

Working towards long-term goals with a long-term mindset means that you and your team can relate to the overall mission without worrying about small failures along the way (Byrd, 2020). Accepting failure and success builds resilience in the team. If you are a leader with a long-term mindset, then your emotional maturity is your core strength and helps you take on challenges quite readily. Psychological safety is quite apparent in the long-term mindset.

Therefore, effective leadership is all about expanding your mind to imbibe positivity (Gottfredson, 2018). You may possess a mindset of your own, and you want to prime your mindset towards an improved way of thinking. This is the essence of being an effective leader.

Why Positivity is Integral to Great Leadership

What makes leadership so vital to organizational success? It is a complicated idea spanning beyond mere micromanagement. Leading people positively is effective and impactful. It means extraordinarily positive performance, orientation towards strengths rather than weaknesses, and the promotion of positive values such as moral integrity and virtue (Cameron, 2008).

Positive leadership is several notches above being a good leader. As Ackerman (2019) puts it, if you can imagine a leadership bell curve with positive leadership behaviors to the right and negative behaviors to the left, then the middle portion of the bell curve is where most leadership behaviors occur.

In developing a positive leadership style, the goal is to shift the behavior to the far right of this curve. Positive leadership is about enhancing positive emotions, promoting "employee development", developing "optimism", "integrity", and high "self-awareness" (Avolio and Gardner, 2005).

At an organizational level, it fosters behaviors such as commitment, loyalty, and positive change management. Avolio and Gardner (2005) expand their idea further to describe authentic leadership, which is governed by relationship transparency, balanced processing, internalized moral perspective, and self-awareness.

Closely related to their idea are several other similar leadership styles:

- Transformational leadership, as defined by Bass and Riggio (2006), consists of "inspirational motivation", that is about the leader inspiring and motivating his followers, "intellectual stimulation" that acts as a drive for innovation and activity, "idealized influence", which makes the leader respected by his followers, and "individualized consideration", which makes the leader treat his or her followers as unique with their individual weaknesses and strengths.

Closely related to the transformational leadership style is the charismatic style which makes the leaders competent at communicating on a deeper level.

- Intelligence expert, Daniel Goleman identifies four styles of leadership, which are coaching leaders (foster team development), democratic leaders (collaborate and pool information to make decisions), affiliative leaders (excel at conflict resolution and promoting harmony), and visionary leaders (with an ambitious vision, always ready to inspire others to chase the vision).

- Leaders may also employ the servant leadership style, which is all about empowering the team, directing them, and expressing interpersonal acceptance, humility, authenticity, and stewardship.

On the whole, positive leadership is all about care, support, empowerment, and compassion. As a positive leader, you may find yourself trying to understand mistakes, guiding your followers, and providing resources. Emotional stability, confidence, good self-esteem, self-efficacy, and locus of control are the traits that propel you as a positive leader. Youssef and Luthans (2012) point out that resilient leaders are better problem-solvers and more competent.

To be an effective positive leader, you need specific behavioral traits for your future success. These traits are about behaving transparently, being trustworthy, supportive, empowering, and self-aware. It is also about displaying ethical behavior (Ackerman, 2019). Reh (2020) explains that positive leadership is all about being able to share enthusiasm, motivating the team, keeping negativity out, and being always productive, always positive.

Why It's Important for Leaders to be Able to Cast Vision

As a leader, it is highly desirable to be able to look forward or have a vision. Not only that, it is also important to communicate this vision to the team so they can see your vision as clearly. Having a vision and communicating it gives two options - to pursue the intended direction or choose the other one. Vision is all about knowing where the organization was in the past, its present state, and where it will be in the future. Vision heavily depends on values and a joint effort.

Effective leaders must be able to cast vision clearly and loudly, involve people, their feedback and message, define a purpose and meaning, and give your vision a personal touch so everyone feels like they have made a contribution. Finally, there will be ups and downs and the key is to maintain resilience.

Chapter Summary

- The wrong leadership mindsets hurt your experiences.
- If you have a fixed mindset, you may think that individuals do not change, and give up easily.
- A performance mindset makes you avoid negative judgments, and you are neither adaptable nor cooperative.

- An implemental mindset makes you a bad decision-maker.
- A prevention mindset leads you into avoiding problems, influencing your performance and innovation.
- An inward mindset makes you regard people as objects, leading you into accusing others when things do not work in your favor.
- An independent mindset leaves you worried about your own prosperity, making it difficult to build trust.
- The key to leadership success is having the right mindset.
- A growth mindset encourages you to seek knowledge and meet your goals most of the time.
- A learning mindset encourages you to expand your competence, making you a high performer.
- A winning mindset is oriented towards gains and winning, and encourages innovation.
- Leaders with deliberative mindsets are good decision-makers.
- An outward mindset makes you value the people around you, and introspect about problems.
- An interdependent mindset promotes cohesiveness within the team.
- Leaders with curious mindsets learn from failures and use them to succeed in future.
- Positivity is an essential aspect of great leadership.
- Positive leadership is all about optimism, self-awareness, integrity, and employee development.
- There are several effective leadership styles including transformational leadership, servant leadership, charismatic leadership, visionary leadership, and many more.
- Leaders must be able to cast vision by understanding the organization, as it was in the past, the present, and in the future, communicate that vision, and make the team feel involved.

Chapter Two: Say:Do Ratio

Back to David and Goliath, and it's all about the say:do ratio this time. David makes realistic promises and lives up to his promises with a humble attitude. He wins the trust of his team as well as clients. David has a positive or high say:do ratio. On the converse side, Goliath sets unrealistic expectations and does not care to follow through. His team is quite dissatisfied with his attitude and the organization sustains heavy losses and a high attrition rate. Here's what happens …

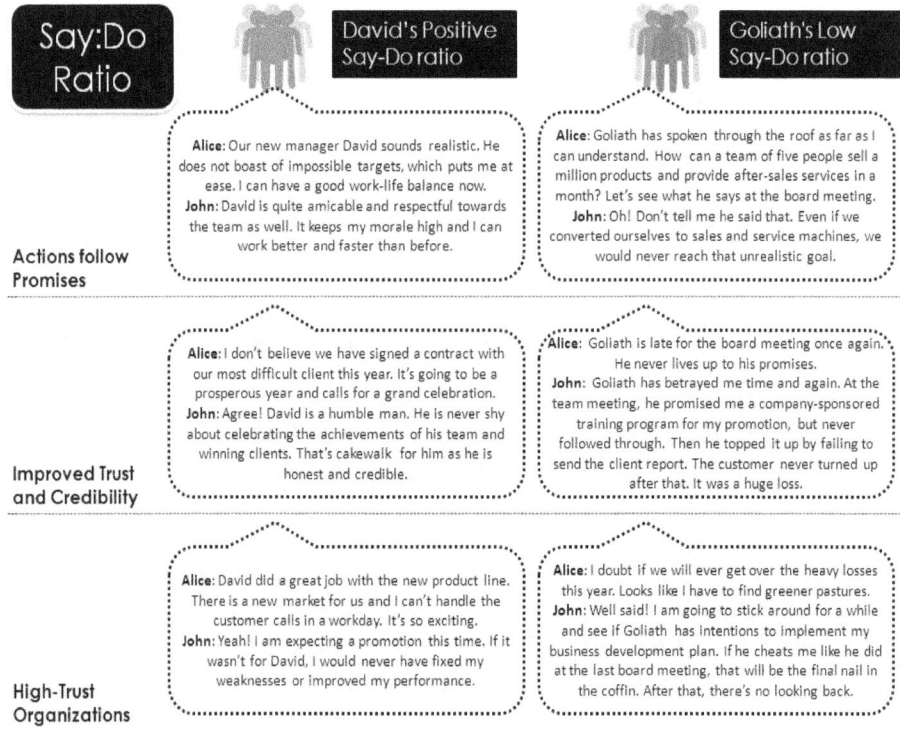

What Is the Say:Do Ratio

The "Say-Do" gap is simply described as something that measures how much you "practice what you preach". In other words, it tells whether your "Visible actions" follow your "stated promises". The closer this relation, the narrower your "say:do" gap. When managers do not show an action for what they have stated, they end up agitating everyone in the office, and also raise doubts about their leadership (Deeb, 2019). When employees are no longer able to trust the credibility of a leader, their loyalty is seriously damaged. This often depicts a wide say-do gap and gives rise to high employee turnover and low morale in the office.

Chapiewski (2020) describes the say-do ratio in different ways: "doing what you committed", "following on your tasks without someone reminding", "prioritizing your tasks" so you can "consistently and reliably deliver", and "doing things on time". The author indicates that the say-do ratio is an indicator of your "responsibility", "reliability", and "self-management".

It would be best if there is a decent say: do proportion. On the off chance that you say a particular something, and do it, you will have a 1:1 say-do proportion. Leaders with an ideal ratio such as 1:1 or something close to it are perceived as more "competent, reliable, trustworthy, and consistent". If you guarantee to complete three things and do everything, your proportion will be adjusted to 3:3. This means that you still have a say-do ratio of 1:1 (Chapiewski, 2020). In another case, when you guarantee to complete five things and you do only a few of them, then your proportion will not be adjusted. It remains 5:2, which may not be considered an ideal say-do ratio, and inevitably leads to negative perceptions.

Why Is the Say:Do Gap Important

A reasonable say vs. do proportion (say: do) is one of the characteristics that speaks volumes about leadership, and a narrow say-do ratio puts them in the category of extraordinary leaders (Chapiewski, 2020). The following scenarios describe contrasting instances of say-do ratios and how the perceptions of employees about their leaders, and, therefore, their attitudes and behaviors vary drastically.

Deeb (2019) describes a wide say-do gap case study in an example describing work at Red Rocket. In this case, there is a good rapport of the subordinates with their CEO in the beginning. However, the management says they can fix a problem and claim they have the resources to accomplish their task, but they do not actually fix the problem. The author indicates that they do not show any intention to solve the problem which reduces the trust and credibility the employees hold for their management. The author admits that there may be several concerns, including dilution of ownership from financing, the management being debt-averse, their preference to avoid conflict, or any form of disagreement with the recommendations of their team. All these scenarios cause initial excitement, which ends up in disappointment eventually when the expected action is not taken.

In another example, Deeb (2019) explains a narrow say-do gap in the case of iExplore at a time when the travel business was adversely affected because of the 9/11 incident that took place in 2001. Honesty with the team regardless of the scenario meant that the promises were always followed through. For example, when the employees are told that the company would raise fresh capital or that it would enter into a new partnership, the relevant action is always taken.

Keeping up the promises led to increased trust, which lasted even in times of crisis. The narrow say-do gap led to unexpected benefits in a time of crisis. Even when revenues declined considerably, burn rates increased, and many employees had to be terminated, the trust built over time caused many employees to volunteer over a period of three months to assist in raising new capital (Deeb, 2019). A similar effort is generally extremely difficult in most other companies, but the trust built over time made a positive change at iExplore. The effort contributed by the management and employees saved the company, and it was due to the narrow say-do gap that helped maintain the trust in the leader. This trust contributed to the combined team effort and helped the company in a time of crisis.

The above scenarios state two extreme instances of the say-do gap to explain why it is followed- through what you say to your team. When there is trust and your team views you as credible, it is easy to move mountains. Maintaining a narrow say-do say gap acts as a form of contingency planning in times of crisis when you can count on the much-needed support from your team as they are willing to go out of the way and build what may be lacking to get back to a flawless state.

How to Intentionally Ensure You are Following Through

<u>What Behaviors Could Lead to a Wide Say-Do Gap</u>

Chapiewski (2020) talks about "anti-patterns" such as "talking up", which refers to the practice of talking about something but not executing it and ending up with a bad say-do ratio. This practice is often quite closely related to exaggerating, or sometimes, even lying. This is a sure path to losing credibility as people may even stop believing you. "Emotional promises" is another such pattern that refers to a state when a person makes a promise but is unable to fulfill it. Such a pattern may make people feel that you are not serious about your work or cannot live up to your promises. It is, therefore, important to stay away from these anti-patterns to be able to achieve a narrow say-do gap or even an ideal say-do ratio.

How to Intentionally Achieve a Narrow Say-Do Gap

A definite way to improve credibility by narrowing down the say-do gap is to "under-promise" and "over-deliver". This happens when a leader sets "reasonable expectations" but strives to better than what was promised, improving performance considerably. The other way to improve your say-do ratio is by way of humility while also working on the essential qualities of confidence and modesty and also boosting one's self-esteem. Chapiewski (2020) recommends a third pattern to improve on the say-do ratio, which he refers to as "quiet benevolence", which simply means doing something good or constructive and remaining quiet about it. People invariably end up acknowledging the difference it made to them, boosting your credibility and improving your say-do ratio.

Understanding Different Personalities for a Narrow Say-Do Gap

Leadership is a challenging game. A leader must be in a position to tackle a wide range of situations including handling superiors and employees, setting up milestones, and getting the right kind of support to be an effective leader (Sluss, 2020). At the outset, you are more likely to have the confidence of your bosses, but the confidence from your team must be built consciously and a formal title of leadership is seldom the only criteria to gain the confidence of your subordinates.

Employees are willing to invest trust in their leaders for differing reasons. Some individuals find it important for the leader to know the core characteristics of the job. This quality may be a critical aspect to be able to support the decisions taken by the leader (Sluss, 2020). A certain survey targeted at understanding the preferences and perceptions of employees classified this category as "warriors" and their chief characteristic was their tendency to evaluate the capabilities, knowledge, approach, and experience to make a choice to support them. "Warriors" explained that this type of evaluation was important for them as they wanted to avoid the problems they had faced in the past.

On the other hand, "warriors" sought security from the new leader in terms of communicating job expectations, future plans, and steps required to accomplish specific processes. Warriors seemed meticulous about choosing their leaders as they wanted to find out all about the leader's policies, approaches, and style of supervision (Sluss, 2020). Leaders are expected to cater to the expectations of both types of employees.

In general, experts believe that relationships with supervisors could provide the necessary motivation to form amicable relations with peers, foster creativity, and identify oneself with the company (Sluss, 2020). The trust inculcated by the leader forms the foundation for high morale and teamwork. Some employees also felt that it was possible to bond well with leaders and relate with them when they shared personal details and narrated their opinion about their job.

<u>Tips for Leaders to Follow through on their Stated Promises</u>

New leaders can make a positive difference by following simple strategies to achieve an ideal say-do ratio:

- Work on improving your relationship with your direct reports as it helps to boost morale and foster teamwork. It also encourages creativity (Sluss, 2020). A good way to relate to a person is to attempt to find out something about their personal interests to be able to bond well.
- Make an effort to inform your subordinates about the story of your career (Sluss, 2020). Sharing a story about your experiences to create a good impression about yourself and garner their trust in you.
- Building trust is all about integrity (Peterson, 2020). Leaders must be extremely careful about results delivered, assess

expectations, and build "high-trust organizations". High-trust organizations happen when leaders set standards, acknowledge less expected contributions, and encourage participation from team members.
- Saying "yes" to everything is also detrimental to your positive say-do ratio as it raises the risk of not following through on your promises. Effective leaders must say "no" when appropriate to manage expectations well (Debevoise, 2020). This strategy also prevents burnout from having to follow through with a multitude of hard-to-handle tasks. In addition, learning when to say "no" protects your emotional and financial health as you no longer operate on a low say-do ratio.

In effect, a sense of accountability in a leader drives a positive say-do ratio, which is the foundation for trust and fosters authenticity and credibility. A positive say-do ratio is the force behind collaborative effort. On the converse side, a low say-do ratio or wide say-do gap may give rise to suspicion and loss of credibility (Debevoise, 2020). Therefore, aligning with the expectations of people is an important part of effective leadership.

Chapter Summary

- Say:do ratio measures how much you practice what you preach as a leader.
- The say:do ratio indicates three important aspects: reliability, responsibility, and self-management.
- When you do what you say, your say:do ratio will be 1:1. Likewise when you promise three things and complete all of them, your say:do ratio will be 3:3.
- A wide say:do gap leads to less credibility and trust, and numerous adverse effects.

- A narrow say:do gap provides unexpected benefits in crisis due to the trust built over time.
  - A narrow say:do gap can be intentionally achieved when you under-promise and over-deliver.
  - Other strategies include boosting self-esteem and increasing humility.
  - Quiet benevolence is another strategy, when you remain silent after doing something constructive.
  - To achieve an ideal say:do ratio, leaders can improve their relationship with subordinates, talk about their career, build integrity, and agree to do something after reflection.
  - A positive say:do ratio is built on trust, which relates to credibility and authenticity.

Chapter Three: Communicating Success

Goliath can't stop fidgeting at the team meeting. He doesn't have any idea how the company performed in the last quarter, and can't get along with two of his star performers. Their senior manager intervenes to dissipate the unnecessarily building tension between Goliath and the team members. The team settles down finally, and David is invited to present the quarterly performance report. His team appears composed and there is a certain harmony in the way they carry themselves. David adjusts his tie, gives the audience a broad smile, and walks up to the desk to present at the team meeting …

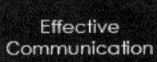

Effective Communication

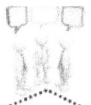

David's Leadership Communication

Goliath's Bad Communication

Good Communication

… is all about Building Trust

… with Two-Way Discourses

… that add Value

… and the Use of Effective Body Language

David: Hello team! I am delighted to present to you the excellent performance of our team during the last quarter. Our company has made it to the Gartner's Magic Quadrant for Cloud Applications. We happen to be the "Leaders".

[A standing ovation and cheerful remarks from the team. David shakes hands and presents a thank you note and chocolate to the team members]

Alice: We always knew you could get us here, David. A quick question, I'm just curious.

David: Absolutely. Please shoot.

Alice: What were our key strengths that made us to the "Leaders" quadrant?

David: Thanks you Alice, for your interest. Well, it was to do with the comprehensive roadmap. Thanks to John for the timely information on that subject. Our products capabilities are also a notch ahead of most competitors in our market space. Moreover, we have a comprehensive product vision. Do you think there's anything more for next time?

Alice: I think it couldn't get better than this! [Alice is all smiles]

David: Over to Goliath for the KPIs

[Goliath sighs in despair. He has no idea where the company is heading. He has never once looked at anything that relates to the performance of the company or stakeholders].

Goliath: I want you all to take this assessment and turn it in 5 minutes. I will not entertain any delays. No questions asked.

Alice: Goliath, the fifth … [Goliath interrupts Alice in the middle of her question. Alice is silent and resentful, but does not communicate her feelings.]

Goliath: Alice, how many times have I made it clear at the team meetings that I don't like to be asked questions in the middle of an assessment.

Alice: Sorry about that, Goliath.

John: Alice, take it easy. I had seen him the day before and he looked lost in the quarterly performance stats. I sat there for 20 minutes, waiting for the first few milestones to include in the roadmap. But he did not budge. It's clear. The graph made no sense to him.

Alice: It's not something he can imbibe in a day or two. Company performance is something he needs to follow over months. God help Goliath!

Leadership communication is integral to the success of businesses. Only those leaders who are successful in learning the right communication skills can drive business results. Effective leaders do this by providing their team with the opportunities and tools that are important to have meaningful conversations. Leaders must plan a way to relate the story of a company's culture and values to stakeholders, to be able to influence the vision and mission of an organization (Jouany & Martic, 2021). When you communicate with your team, you build the essential aspects of trust, productivity, satisfaction, and motivation.

A leader who imbibes good communication is successful in creating a connected workplace. Effective communicators are able to help their team identify themselves with the company culture and strategy (Jouany & Martic, 2021). They encourage employee engagement through two-way conversations, keep them informed and enforce collaboration. They are also able to prevent miscommunications within the organization and are able to manage change.

Statistical insights back up these traits of effective communicators. Gallup's survey on the "State of the American Workplace" indicates that a lack of engagement among 70% of the employees leads to $450-$550 billion productivity losses annually (Napolitano, 2016). Branham (n.d.), in his article on "The 7 hidden reasons employees" indicates that a lack of coaching and feedback led to a decline in performance, and that yearly performance appraisals were not as effective. Yelling, screaming, and threatening (YST) were, unfortunately, a prominent form of miscommunication and employees complained that they did not receive honest feedback from their managers. The author indicated the need for an "adult-to-adult partnership" between a manager and an employee and recommended the use of "upward evaluations" to enable employees to anonymously rate their managers.

A Project.co report on communication statistics details several sections related to productivity, task and project management, productivity at work, and communication channels. The survey insights indicate that email is the primary means for communication with clients for 65% of businesses, while 16% use online tools. Email communication between coworkers was limited to 39% of the employees and 28% of coworkers used online tools for communication. Good communication was extremely important for clients as 74% indicated that they moved to a competitor as they felt that the business was disorganized. Further, 29% of the employees indicated that they used online project management tools. It was interesting to note that while 89% of the survey participants indicated the importance of effective communication, "8 out of 10" people believed that their communication was either average or poor. Also, online communication tools made the employees rate their organization, efficiency levels, and communication as "excellent" (Project.co, 2020).

Workforce research indicates that when internal communication is poor, employees suffer from low morale, losses in productivity, and employee turnover is quite high. Besides, poor internal communication adversely affects the company's bottom line (Jensen, 2019). Surveys have indicated that communication is an essential aspect of team building. When open and honest communication was missing, employee morale suffered profoundly. The solution to the problem of low morale was to keep employees in the loop about company goals and performance, provide timely feedback, and encourage their queries (www.recruiter.com, 2013).

Furthermore, the Kenexa Research Institute survey on employee opinion from 25,000 employees present globally indicated that employee engagement was a key driver for employee retention, job satisfaction, and advocacy, which promoted a positive organizational culture, and employees were observed to be less engaged when future was uncertain, their co-workers were not motivated, and their contribution was not recognized (*Kenexa Research Institute announces world rankings for employee engagement*, 2009). Moreover, experts at the Korn Ferry Hay Group recommended that managers follow certain strategies during change to keep their employees engaged: making communication extremely clear, engaging the employees prior to change, assisting leaders in understanding their role in change, trying ways to retain talented employees, ensuring managers have the tools and skills to engage teams (Ferry, 2016).

According to the "State of Miscommunication" survey carried out by Quantum Workplace and Fierce Conversations, the perceptions on miscommunication from 1,300 employees indicated that only half as many conversations about their work were high quality, and only 47.5% of the employees stated their opinion frankly. More than 80% of the employees indicated that miscommunication was a frequent occurrence at the workplace. The majority of the survey participants (52.7%) thought that all employee groups were to be blamed for the miscommunication, and about 32.5% of them believed that their superiors were responsible. Other factors that could be traced to miscommunication were technology such as email or phone, and group meetings (Gentle, 2017).

Examples of Poor Communication

While good communication is the cornerstone of effective leadership, with leaders being able to gain trust and respect from their peers, and encouraging creativity, bad communication is at the root of "organizational chaos". The following examples illustrate instances of poor communication (Write, n.d.).

- Leadership communication that does not have clarity can make the team feel frustrated and cause them to lose motivation.
- When leaders are not able to communicate the goals of the company, they leave the team with false expectations and uncertainty.
- If a leader is not willing to listen to the problems of employees, no matter how insignificant they may be, the latter may feel unhappy and contemplate leaving the workplace.
- Boasting is never perceived as positive by employees, and being humble goes a long way in fostering effective communication and overall business success.
- Conveying information too late and making employees anxious about the next steps accounts for bad leadership.
- Leaders who take all credit for whatever positive happens will eventually leave the employees feeling frustrated and resentful. The same goes with not being able to take on the responsibility for one's actions when things go wrong.

Practices to Improve Communication and Expectations

Based on insights from several credible sources, Harvard Business School Online put together important insights on the rationale behind incorporating effective communication in leadership (Landry, 2019). First, to be an effective leader, you need to "excel in communication". As statistics indicate, poor communication is the root cause of several other problems including missed performance goals, low sales, and low morale. Ineffective communication was clearly associated with high costs. On the converse side, effective communication was the key to employee empowerment, shared vision, increased trust, and successful organizational change.

As an effective leader, the most important aspect you want to influence by communicating well is to initiate increment and positive change and empower employees. This is the path to gaining trust and preventing misinterpretation of information, preventing barriers and negative relationships, and impediments to progress (Landry, 2019). In order to achieve these outcomes, you want to focus on key communication skills for leadership success:

Adapt a Communication Style That Has a Positive Impact

To be able to adopt a good communication style, you want to first assess your leadership style. This strategy for self-assessment is essential as it defines your future interactions with employees and their perceptions about your capabilities (Landry, 2019). Employees are motivated for different reasons, and an effective leader is able to adapt effortlessly to come down to the level of individual employees towards the achievement of organizational goals.

Know When to Talk and When to Listen

Listen intently to employee opinions and ideas, and implement their feedback with a positive attitude. Encourage engaging conversations with employees when they share feedback by asking questions, noting down their feedback, and asking them to explain in detail. You want to keep conversations polite and abstain from interrupting and make employees feel important (Landry, 2019). Finally, avoid distractions, and keep your email and mobile phone offline to achieve a good rhythm during the conversation and promote good team bonding.

Maintain Transparency and Clarity in Communication

One of the essential aspects of effective leadership is to have a clear understanding of what is happening within the organization. If you are able to identify yourself with the opportunities, challenges faced by the organization, and have a shared vision and goals, then you will be able to communicate beyond common barriers and empower employees to collaborate and solve problems. Furthermore, you want to be specific about what you want to communicate with your employees (Landry, 2019). By defining the outcomes related to strategic goals and associated milestones, you will be able to clear out any confusion in the early stages when your project is about to take off. In doing so, you are able to provide a clear picture about the tasks to employees involved in the task or project, or precisely engage them right from the start.

Ask Questions and Show Empathy

Asking questions is an effective approach to understanding the goals, motivations, and thought processes of employees. Leaders who frequently ask open-ended questions such as "Can you please elaborate?", "Can you please explain this in greater detail", or "Could you please define that term more clearly?" you can get your team to think in-depth about the question being asked and frame an appropriate response (Landry, 2019). In doing so, you are better equipped with the requirements of your employees and have a higher chance of succeeding in your endeavors.

Furthermore, empathy is an integral part of leadership success. Empathy ensures that a leader has a good understanding of his or her teammates and is able to make sense of their experiences and feelings. It ensures greater connectedness among team members. Employees feel valued for their contributions, and leaders who practice empathy are able to build a strong culture that fosters productivity. Parmar (2016) writes that the 2016 Empathy Index linked empathy to productivity, growth, and earnings per employee. The research survey found that ethics and empathy were closely related, and top companies like Microsoft and Facebook top the list of empathetic companies. Furthermore, empathy is closely related to ethics given the rising number of scandals in the corporate world and the data from the National Business Ethics survey. Furthermore, leadership assessments carried out by the Management Research Group (MRG) indicated that empathy was the strongest predictor of ethics-based leadership. In this review, Dowden (2013) recommends that leading by example, rewarding employees based on empathy, and hiring new talent on the basis of empathy among other factors help to build an empathetic organization.

<u>Maintain Open Body Language</u>

Non-verbal cues are as important to effective leaders as they are in any other form of communication. A focus on body language goes a long way in inspiring employees and giving them the right message. Some of the non-verbal cues that help establish positive connections with your employees include making eye contact and smiling. While these cues convey trust, gestures like clenched fists convey the wrong message and may inhibit their interest in forming a healthy bond.

Goman (2018) indicates several interesting aspects of body language such as your ability to make an impact with non-verbal cues in less than seven seconds, the use of hands to place emphasis on what you are trying to say, influencing and building trust with face-to-face communication, and the usefulness of being able to read body language. When you make a first impression with your body language, your team begins to view you through filters such as "trustworthiness" or "power". Another important aspect of building trust is to have a good alignment between your body language and what you are saying, as the converse projects negative aspects like internal conflict and uncertainty. Furthermore, face-to-face communication is one of the most effective forms of communication as it triggers mirror neurons, which leads to the mimicking of sensations, feelings, and behaviors. Finally, by reading the body language of your team members, you are able to discern between their engagement and disengagement.

What Gets Measured Gets Done

The trait of good communication can be measured in terms of a high degree of "situational and contextual awareness". Communicating well also requires you to be an effective observer and listener (Myatt, 2012). The following principles can serve as golden rules when communicating with your team:

- Effective leaders communicate clearly. Communication that is concise, brief, and simple is critical to make your team understand what you are trying to put across to them.
- Listen well, encourage conversations as opposed to a monologue, and make your team interactions enjoyable discourses.
- Whet your skills often and gain expertise in your subject to be able to add value to every conversation you have with your team.
- Stay alert with sharp reflexes during team interactions, so that when your words and actions do not seem to have the desired effect, you are able to imbibe what the situation demands and make the required changes to your message.
- Be an empathetic communicator and display authenticity as opposed to arrogance during conversations.
- Be open to a wide range of opinions even though the views of your team may come as confrontational or challenging.
- Keep your communications personal so as to engage your team and develop meaningful relationships and understand what goes on in their minds.
- Make it your priority to earn the trust of your employees by the way you think and act, so that when they perceive you as worthy of your trust, they are willing to invest their time and take risks for higher goals.
- Make your communication a means of getting access to information, exchanging ideas, understanding expectations,

guiding the team to take action, and realizing the vision of the company.

That said, measuring performance is a key aspect of business success. Most organizations refer to these measurements as Key Performance Indicators (KPIs) as these metrics are aligned to business objectives (Wishart, 2019). Simply put, KPIs help you achieve the desired results. An organization requires KPIs for many reasons beyond monitoring the health of the company. KPIs help analyze patterns, provide information to make the necessary adjustments, solve problems, and measure progress in an organization.

To elaborate, the four aspects that need to be measured in any organization are customers, revenue, processes, and employees. Company progress may be measured by monitoring revenue, the number of employees, gross margin. KPIs, such as the number of interested customers, number of outbound calls, and number of appointments help understand opportunities and solve problems. (Wishart, 2019). Furthermore, many businesses use KPIs to analyze patterns for each quarter and make future predictions. Keeping yourself in the loop about how the various KPIs are performing helps you communicate the right message and create the right impact. It also drives your actions to improve your organizational performance and understand the progress of employees.

Cadence

Leadership communication happens through different channels and in many ways. The key points pertaining to leadership communication are included below (*Leadership & Cadence: Communication -- More than Just Words*, n.d.):

- Effective leaders spend time in assessing what exactly is being communicated and the person and time related to this communication. Sometimes, messages need to be communicated to only a specific group of employees, such as in the case of layoffs, and in other cases, the message may be included in between meetings.
- Most businesses rely on both formal (printed newsletters, policy, or memo) and informal (socializing and talking to employees) means of communication.
- Communications must be accompanied by continued follow-ups. To-way communications are effective as they factor in valuable employee feedback. Furthermore, updates must happen regularly such as on a weekly on monthly basis.
- Leaders must take feedback regularly and get accurate information before addressing the team to keep them motivated.
- Different types of communications are delivered by different people belonging to the organization. For example, employee performance may be conveyed by a supervisor, updates on business operations may be delivered by the manager or a senior leader, and a larger event such as restructuring may be delivered by a senior executive in the organization.
- Employee feedback on communication channels is integral to leadership success. Informal forums may be set up to obtain the opinion of staff.

As a leader, it is critical to be on the lookout for opportunities to communicate with your team members. This is an important strategy as it ensures your success in the short-term and long run. Experts suggest that creating a communication cadence achieves this goal for you and your team (Eikenberry, 2019). Establishing a rhythm in communicating with your team members is all about building cadence with your team to be effective as a leader. Planning with the participation of your team is the path to a prudent plan for communication cadence. There are a few key areas to focus on to come up with a good plan for communication cadence:

- Understand the individual needs and preferences of your team members to hone in on the right cadence. Factor in the individual competencies, communication frequencies, and work profiles.
- Organizations suffer from poor communication more often than not, and you want to look at all the informal issues that we will come across during the workday.
- Give as much importance to the needs of your team members as your own preferences before creating a plan for communication cadence.
- Plan for one-on-one communication with every team member by establishing a weekly schedule, with a proper list of things to discuss, backed by an agenda.
- Also discuss the bigger picture with your team members such as career planning and goals on a less frequent, but regular basis, such as on a quarterly basis to maintain the cadence.

Finally, considering the communication priorities discussed in the chapter, it is important to mention that in the wake of the COVID-19 crisis, strong leaders must possess the essential qualities of being accessible, providing video updates, creating cadence by enforcing consistency and clarity, displaying resilience, kindness, persistence, and calmness, and listening to your staff for business success (Leonard, 2020).

Chapter Summary

- Leaders need the right communication skills to drive business results.

- Communication is essential to win the trust of employees, make them productive, and keep them motivated and satisfied.
- Good communication skills are essential for collaboration and change management.
- Poor internal communication leads to productivity loss, low morale, and high employee turnover.
- Engaging employees improves retention rates, increases job satisfaction, and promotes a positive organizational culture.
- Poor communication leads to frustration, low motivation, uncertainty, and resentment.
- Good communication requires adaptability, transparency, good listening skills, empathy, and open body language.
- Leaders must build a rhythm in communication, or build cadence.
- To create a good plan for communication cadence, understand the preferences of the team, identify informal issues, and plan one-to-one communication.

Chapter Four: Consistent Feedback Culture

David is a great manager, always appreciating his team members for their good work. He specifically acknowledges their achievements and how it has a positive effect on the company. His team reciprocates by giving the required information in a timely manner. Whenever there is a problem, David is careful about not being overly critical and makes sure his criticism is accompanied by letting his team members know how valuable they are for the company. On the other hand, Goliath has not learned enough about keeping his best employees happy. He is outright critical most of the time, which leaves his team members dissatisfied. Here's the story of a striking contrast in feedback styles ...

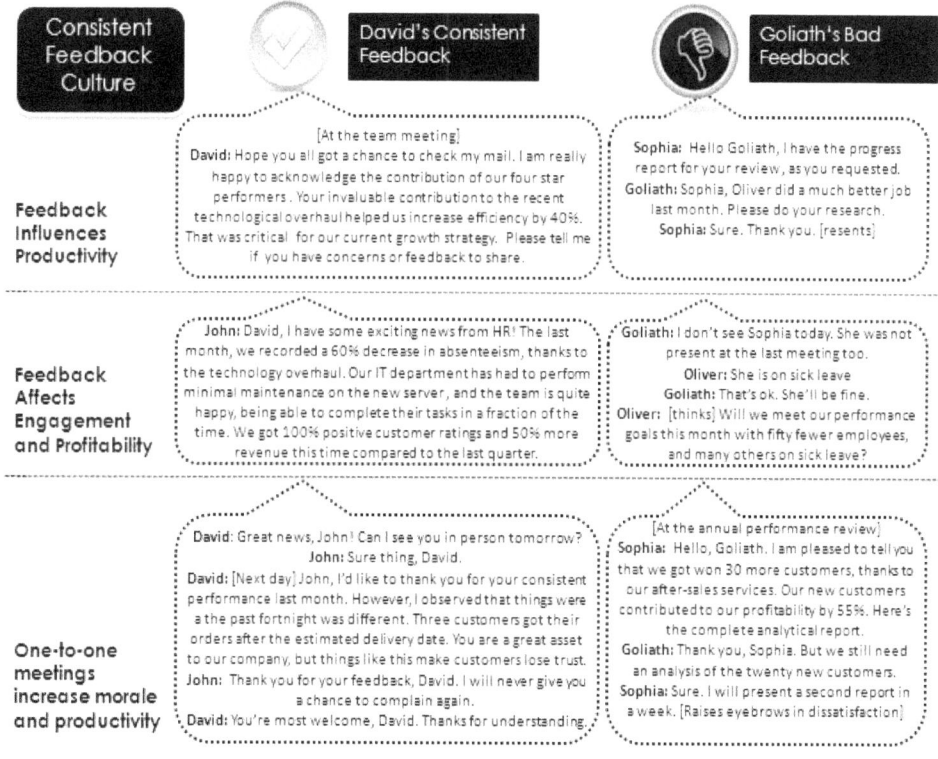

The Need for a Consistent Feedback Culture

Culture is an important aspect of a company and is based on organizational values. It affects performance and influences how tasks are accomplished in an organization. Culture also influences the thinking and behavior of employees and defines how they work in the company (*Bad Company Culture Definition and Its Impact*, 2019). Culture may not necessarily align with the strategy of your company. Certain cultures are good for the workforce while others are not.

Companies that foster a positive culture are characterized by high performance, high engagement of employees, and leaders who are a reflection of the company values and hold themselves accountable for their actions. There are certain good and bad aspects of cultures that become clearly apparent. Companies with bad cultures often feature interpersonal conflict, suboptimal performance, and a high degree of discrimination (*Bad Company Culture Definition and Its Impact*, 2019). Bad cultures not just affect employees and the bottom line, but factors that lie beyond that as a lack of accountability means an absence of ethical behavior that has a negative influence on the customers of the company.

The Profound Impacts of Bad company Culture

An example of bad company culture is 3M, a company that produced Teflon pans regarded as toxic for humans, animals, and the environment. In spite of being aware of the consequences of the chemical toxicity, the company continued to produce their product as their workplace culture was toxic and employees did not feel the much-needed sense of responsibility (*Bad Company Culture Definition and Its Impact*, 2019). These unethical practices were banned due to the efforts of the Environmental Protection Agency after almost four decades, which was quite an elaborate time frame, the result of a lack of accountability on part of the company. The example of 3M demonstrates that cooperation, truth, and openness are important aspects of workplace culture.

The Why and How of Encouraging Positive Feedback Culture

Therefore, it is important to extend considerable effort towards fostering a feedback culture that encourages regular participation from employees. The nature of feedback is very important to achieve desired results. The intent of a feedback exercise should be to learn as opposed to disciplining employees (*"How Much?" Here's Why You Should Invest in Feedback Culture*, n.d.). This approach is more likely to encourage constructive and positive feedback. The nature of feedback is top-down as opposed to multi-directional. A positive approach to constructive feedback is retaining employees and boosting their productivity.

While transitioning from a system of annual performance appraisals to a regular feedback system that relies on rapid information exchange and communication, the nature of feedback systems must also adapt accordingly. Employees are expected to master their skills faster, projects are expected to adhere to shorter timelines, job requirements are constantly revised, and the millennials dominate the workforce (*"How Much?" Here's Why You Should Invest in Feedback Culture*, n.d.). In this type of setup, annual performance reviews are outdated mechanisms that feature dissatisfaction from managers and a lack of correlation between business results and annual performance ratings. On the contrary, continuous feedback systems provide faster and more meaningful results in an age of rapid changes in business structure and function. Studies have indicated that regular feedback can bring about a decline in absenteeism (41%) and employee turnover (59%), and enhance the performance of employees (39%) as well as the effectiveness of leadership (71%). Continuous feedback also has positive effects on profitability and customer ratings (*"How Much?" Here's Why You Should Invest in Feedback Culture*, n.d.).

Experts believe that consistent feedback leads to marked productivity gains. A company with 200 employees and an annual revenue of 15 million Euros in the form of an annual revenue may be able to benefit by as much as 5-6 million Euros in the form of productivity and savings by improving feedback culture. Moreover, forward-thinking organizations are constantly engaged in retaining and developing employee potential, and this is reinforced by almost 90% of leaders who are innovators (*"How Much?" Here's Why You Should Invest in Feedback Culture*, n.d.). Developing employees and productivity is the result of a continuous positive feedback culture in an organization.

The Norm for a Consistent Feedback Culture

To realize substantial improvements in company performance, feedback must not be a part of the company culture, but at the core of its system. Sharing regular feedback is important for a number of reasons (*Why does your company need a strong feedback culture*, n.d.):

- Professional growth and access to regular opportunities in an organization is possible only with a regular feedback culture. This helps employees stay on track with current trends, focus on their strengths and correct their actions to achieve higher standards of performance. Consistent feedback helps notify employees of the areas they need to improve upon in a timely manner. When a leader is able to help the workforce learn and adapt to industry changes, they can give the company a competitive advantage over others.
- Most companies spend a considerable amount of time in manual processes, such as over 200 hours in their annual

performance reviews. However, these reviews are seldom regarded as useful and lead to faulty performance appraisals. Even with a company size as modest as 10,000, the cost an organization may incur as a result of these inefficiencies could be as much as $35 million per year. Rather than depend on an annual performance review, it makes sense to have regular and real-time feedback. As an effective leader, you can encourage regular feedback by encouraging employees to share their thoughts after the completion of tasks or projects that were completed successfully. Gathering this feedback over several months can have a marked positive impact on not just the efficiency of the company but also the bottom line.

- The optimal use of a performance management system for exchanging feedback is the continuous improvement of employee experience. Systems that provide HR metrics can be great tools to exchange individual and team performance feedback, for greater efficiency and satisfaction of the team.
- A strong feedback culture fosters open communication, encourages a positive attitude towards correctional feedback, and helps employees align with company goals. It helps teams build greater trust and rapport.

The Definition of "Good"

Managers can provide useful feedback to the employees through a number of channels beyond year-end appraisals. The primary means of encouraging employees to do better and provide a fair assessment of their strengths and weaknesses is through continuous feedback. Continuous feedback encourages communication among employees and inspires them to meet company goals. It fosters trust among team members (*Why does your company need a strong feedback culture*, n.d.).

Having one-to-one meetings that add value by boosting the morale, productivity, and engagement of the team is a great feedback strategy. These meetings ensure that the team stays focused and serve as a platform to coach and mentor employees using a personalized approach. They are also a reflection of the support an employee is entitled to receive from the leadership. It is important for managers to have an agenda before the meeting. The discussion serves as a crucible to define excellence, and create a plan or roadmap for the success of individual employees. Managers and leaders can adopt several strategies to implement this personalized approach: inquiring about personal goals; identifying challenges for problem-solving; defining expectations; following-up and providing constructive feedback; setting priorities and timelines; identifying where employees showed growth or utilized their strengths; encouraging problem solving; and building strong connections with teams (Hassell, 2017). During one-to-one meetings, it is important to allow employees to express their concerns after the meeting. Ensure that you are not the only one talking. Pause frequently and allow employees to discuss their concerns. Offer assistance in their endeavors and sum up all that happened in the meeting (Austin, 2016).

Dedicated Meetings for Employee Personal Development

The success of personal development reviews depends on the perception of the employees. For example, if the review did not go well in the previous instance, then chances are that the employees will not provide an honest opinion that enhances their productivity. Here are tips to make a personal development review successful for the management and the employees:

- Evaluate your perception and purpose of the one-to-one meetings. What do these meetings mean to you? Are the meetings a platform that helps you and your employees derive value from them? If you are not convinced your current system is set up to address the needs of the management and employees, then it is time to think about the organization of the system and make changes to make the encounter a positive experience for progress and increasing the engagement of employees (Stewart, n.d.).

- Once you have a purpose and an agenda, it is time to focus on the meeting by giving the employees complete attention. Allocate about two hours for the meeting and make sure there are no interruptions. To make the meeting successful, organize the one-to-one personal development review in a meeting room rather than an office that may have distractions from the computer, phone, or other sources. Even when there are unintended or unplanned distractions, make an effort to keep them to a minimum (Stewart, n.d.). For example, if your phone rings, do not pick it up and apologize while keeping your focus on the conversation. This makes your employees feel respected.
- Talk to your employees about not just their performance, but also the performance of the organization and your performance as a manager. Talk to them about the milestones your company has been able to cover as well as any improvements that can be made. During the discussion, make sure you ask them if there is any room for improvement. Keep yourself open to any other discussions that are "off-topic" as it is a good opportunity for them to openly state any issues that they would not want to include in a written report (Stewart, n.d.). As a fair leader, it is your responsibility to advise them if a specific matter needs to be included in the report but without forcing them to do so.
- Continuous feedback when consciously adopted as a practice ensures there are no surprises in the personal development review. If your employees understand that they have been under-performing at this meeting, then there may be a

problem with the nature of feedback, and it is a good idea to make the required amendments (Stewart, n.d.). The personal development review should not be the only review that makes employees vent their frustrations over the last year. If something like this turns out to be the subject of your meetings, then it is time to think again and change the way you communicate with your employees over the next year.

- Sometimes, employees may hesitate to state what is going on and you may not have the required information to make conclusions about their performance. If your employees give very brief answers to you at the meeting, then you may encourage them to speak further by maintaining a brief pause after their answers (Stewart, n.d.). When they perceive you are listening, it may cause them to open up and feel good about providing the required information without being forced to do so.
- Don't be quick to make judgments about the performance of an employee without having adequate information. Sometimes, there may be mishaps or unusual occurrences during the year. These instances should not be regarded as a reflection of the overall performance of employees (Stewart, n.d.). As a leader, you must make fair judgments about their performance by judging how you want to weigh these occurrences. Giving too much importance to these instances may distort the way you view the performance of an employee.
- Make sure you have a proper personalized agenda for every employee for their personal development meetings and state each and every aspect of their performance in a constructive manner in your conversation. It is never a good idea to state a negative aspect in a report without first stating it verbally (Stewart, n.d.). Even in the case when you forgot to state it in the conversation, make it a point to call another brief meeting and explain the same to your employee. When you

are convinced your team member has understood and is able to apply the conclusions in the coming year, then state the facts in the report for it to serve as a reminder. This approach rules out any possibility of confrontation.

How Company Culture is Affected by COVID-19

COVID-19 had a marked impact on company cultures as it reduced face-to-face interaction due to the need for embracing remote work. Although one may expect that the pandemic may have lowered culture ratings, the exact opposite was true for most companies as per ratings from employees. Glassdoor survey ratings indicated that the quality of communication from leaders improved considerably during the pandemic. Employees indicated that leaders were much more transparent and honest in their communication during the pandemic. Companies also scored higher in terms of their integrity as per employee ratings (Sull, 2020).

Employees seemed to be concerned about process complexity, lack of agility, bureaucracy, and lack of entrepreneurship during the course of the pandemic. Employees also indicated that their employer was less flexible in responding to the political unrest, recession, economic uncertainty, and protests during the pandemic period. Employees were also more engaged in discussing diversity, inclusivity, equity, physical and mental well-being, and transparent communication (Sull, 2020). The most common differentiators among top competitive companies were transparency, employee welfare, agility, process flexibility, and communication strategy.

Chapter Summary

- A positive culture features high employee engagement, high performance, and accountability.

- Bad cultures affect the bottom line and influence the customers of the company.
- Regular feedback culture fosters professional growth of employees, efficiency and bottom line of the company, overall team satisfaction, and open communication.
- Personal development reviews are dedicated meetings for employees.
- To make personal development meetings successful, it is important to understand employee perception, make employees feel respected, discuss performance goals and issues, give continuous feedback, encourage employees to share information, have a personalized agenda, and make appropriate judgments about performance.

Chapter Five: Praise & Criticism - When & Where

This story of feedback continues here, as David demonstrates a great example of praising his team member generously before pointing out a small mistake. The result is absolutely positive, with the employee willing to correct himself spontaneously. Goliath is a different type of manager. He often ends up hurting his team members with criticism. He's seldom specific and many-a-time leaves a feedback vacuum. His team member is dissatisfied and hardly motivated to work with a poor boss ...

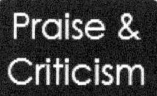  David's Strategy  Goliath's Manner

Use specific and sincere praise in public.

[At the stakeholder meeting]
David: Hey John, your explanatory report was just great. You did a splendid job clarifying the different security issues. We'll implement them next month.
John: Thank you so much, David [smiles cheerfully].

[At John's workstation]
John: [mumbles while making quick calculations] That makes for 30% performance improvement ... here we have another outlier, so trimming down the values we have an overall 50% contribution from IT policy ... and that's it ... a whopping 70% in company growth ...]
David: Hello there, John. All set? I'm so excited to learn more about your comprehensive performance report!
John: Yeah, sure David. All stats in place now. Over to your office in fifteen minutes, if that's okay.
David: Sure John. Looking forward to a great review.
John: [Thumbs up]

Criticize clearly in private

[In David's office]
[John opens up the report in front of David and starts explaining the key statistics. David is impressed]
David: Great job. If it was not for your dedication, we would never get here. Thank you, John. Just one quick feedback. Could you please send in the stats a week ahead of the final reports. It really helps.
John: Oh sure, David. Thanks for letting me know.

Goliath: Oliver, please send your analytical report to my office.
Oliver: Sure, Goliath

[At Goliath's office]
[Oliver is excited about his first presentation. He smiles broadly at Goliath. Oliver starts explaining the report - overall performance, performance by department, customer feedback ... Goliath interrupts]

Goliath: Your figures are so detailed. Do we even need them at this point?

Oliver: Yes Goliath, I think so. They talk about the overall position of the company and how each of the departments performed. Without that information, it will be difficult to conclude how we did during the analysis period.

Goliath: Ok. Whatever. What does this mean, anyway. Did we have a profit or loss?

Oliver: It's not just measuring profit or loss, Goliath. It's much deeper than that.

[Goliath is not listening. Oliver picks up the report, sighs in dismay, and leaves the office]

Kim Scott, in her "Radical Candor" blog, introduces that "being radically candid" is an important aspect of helpful feedback. She further elaborates that when praising someone, it is important to be "specific and sincere". On the other hand, the essential aspects of criticism are being "kind and clear". She further states that this approach helps realize better work relationships and better business results (Scott, n.d.-b). Kim states that the way to go about this is to be "HHIIPP" or ("Humble, Helpful, Immediate, In Person, Private Criticism/Public Praise, Not about Personality").

The Essential Aspects of Effective Feedback

Scott elaborates on each of these six aspects to provide enough information for effective leadership. Being humble in providing feedback means that although you are firm in providing your feedback, you are ready to admit you could be wrong and are ready to imbibe differing perspectives (Scott, n.d.-b). Being curious as opposed to arrogant is important, and your feedback must be supported with a sound rationale. Analyze differing perspectives sufficiently before you decide to either agree or disagree.

Furthermore, when giving feedback, it is important to be helpful by providing clear feedback. It is a good practice to give immediate feedback that is also specific. Moreover, giving in-person feedback is important as it provides an opportunity to understand the reaction of your team member, by closely observing their body language and emotions. Reactions may differ from not hearing you on one extreme to getting upset on the other end (Scott, n.d.-b). A rule of thumb is to criticize in private and praise in public to make your feedback effective. Finally, don't criticize the person directly. Rather, criticize what went wrong to be able to make your feedback beneficial.

The Value of Immediate Feedback

Pandey (2019) discusses "The One Minute Manager" by Blanchard and Johnson. In their work, the authors indicate the value of effective management. The ideal manager described in the book requires very little time to achieve substantial results. He achieves this by one-minute goal setting, which is all about being aware of the expectations from the beginning, deciding the goal and performance level, and recording all of this on a single sheet of paper such that it can be read in a single minute. These one-minute goals are effective as they provide immediate feedback, which motivates the employee. The author states the example of playing a game and the player is aware of the required score and the points scored so far. In this case, the player accurately knows about the results and is motivated to achieve them because he or she has the information. If a player is not aware of the score required to win the game, it is difficult to achieve the desired results. Setting one-minute goals inform the employee exactly what is expected, and it is much easier to measure performance and check on the progress to produce the intended results

There's more to one-minute management, which is observing people when they are doing something right, to be able to praise them instantaneously. In one-minute praise, you have to just take a minute to tell the person that he or she did a great job. This form of immediate praise when you acknowledge the good work of an employee and share the way you feel encourages the person to continue the good work (Pandey, 2019). One minute of praise works over a course of time, and the person being praised feels motivated to perform even better, and his or her performance improves over time. It reflects the care of the leader and concern about their success. In practicing one-minute praise, you must be careful not to criticize every single mistake as it causes the team to abstain from doing wrong, but also does not motivate them to reach higher standards. This results in mediocrity with a reduced possibility of achieving exceptional results. Criticism should be immediate in the form of "one-minute reprimands" as discussed in the section below.

How to Criticise Effectively

Management studies have indicated that positive feedback has a profound impact on the effectiveness of teams. Positive and negative reinforcement is processed by the human brain in different ways. A reward-based approach encourages employees to elevate their performance to higher levels. However, criticism may lead the employees to refrain from doing something that hurts them but does not improve their performance in any way (Cranwell, 2018). As a leader, it is important to understand how and when to criticize. Effective leadership lies in taking the initiative to correct employees when the need arises, but too much criticism may cause low morale and deter employees from reaching their goals.

Maintain a 5:1 Praise: Criticism Ratio for Good Results

The ideal paradise to criticism ratio is 5:1, and this can be achieved by enforcing a few simple strategies. The first step is to understand performance data to identify opportunities when you can praise employees in a timely manner and also address problems as they arise. Customer perspectives in the form of comments and ratings are important sources of information on the quality of your service. (Cranwell, 2018; North, 2019).

To recognize the service delivery of your team members, leaders can encourage them by sending group emails with customer comments to recognize the nature of their performance. Dedicated platforms such as Slack provide a range of options to provide reviews and feedback in a timely manner, that can either enhance performance or address issues as the need arises. Another strategy to encourage healthy competition is by placing a display of employee performance for them to compare and empower each other to drive better and high-quality results. Peer influence often proves as a source of motivation and a lot can be achieved in this way, beyond formal performance management (Cranwell, 2018). While implementing the different strategies to manage the performance of employees, care must be taken to deter from using overly negative approaches as they discourage employee engagement and create difficulties in meeting business goals.

Get Strategic about Negative Corrective Feedback

Evidence indicates that negative feedback has a different "informational value" for experts and novices. This means that novices are likely to receive negative feedback more often than experts based on the assumption that they are more prone to making mistakes. However, this applies only when the scale used to assess the two groups remains the same (Finkelstein & Fishbach, 2012). When a different scale is used to evaluate novices and experts, novices may not perform worse than experts. Researchers cite the example of assessment of piano skills. While novices may be evaluated based on their ability to play different notes correctly, experts may be evaluated on their ability to successfully express emotions using music. In this case, a novice may not necessarily perform worse than an expert.

The value of feedback provided depends entirely on what kind of feedback motivates people. When the feedback is a reflection of commitment and progress towards the goal, it ensures a higher likelihood of success. In this context, negative feedback can be constructive when employees are informed of their progress in relation to expectations and increases motivation. In many cases, the feedback inspired employees to work harder and improve performance. In another instance, the timing of positive and negative feedback defined motivation and performance (Finkelstein & Fishbach, 2012). People on a weight-loss diet who were far from their goals were motivated by positive feedback whose commitment towards their goal increased. On the other hand, those who were close to their goals were motivated by negative feedback as it indicated insufficient progress.

Individuals with different levels of expertise "seek" different types of feedback i.e. negative or positive. They also respond differently to feedback which is manifest in their attitudes and behaviors. Experts find negative feedback meaningful as it increases their motivation to achieve their goals. Novices seek positive feedback and are likely to alter their attitudes and behaviors as a response (Finkelstein & Fishbach, 2012). Moreover, novices get a perception of their commitment from the feedback and experts try to find out if they are good enough in terms of pursuing their goals.

Always Criticize Privately

Criticizing publicly is an ineffective strategy as it makes an individual feel humiliated. An attempt that makes a team member feel embarrassed is bound to put an end to any form of motivation or employee engagement. It is also detrimental to the morale of employees and makes them resentful. Criticism or correcting employee behavior must always be done in private (Tanner, 2020). Only in rare cases, it may be required for a leader to criticize publicly such as when it is imperative to prevent abusive or illegal behavior in the workplace, or when an injury must be prevented. For example, as an effective leader, it may be required to stop offensive behavior in crisis situations by criticizing a specific employee publicly. However, in the majority of cases, private criticism is the strategy that improves employee performance and is also a form of effective leadership.

Private criticism must be done in a kind and clear manner. Being critical about the performance of an employee in public can make it sound harsh. When you criticize your team member in private, it is bound to be more effective as he or she will have their guard down and listen carefully to what you are trying to convey. When they are not defensive, there is a high likelihood of accepting their mistakes and learning from them (Scott, n.d.-a).

Criticize Immediately with a Positive Note

Pandey (2019), in his article, discusses the value of "one-minute reprimands", which is taken from the work of Blanchard and Johnson, entitled "The One Minute Manager". In reprimanding this way, an effective leader tells his team member what went wrong, then let him or her know that they are a valuable asset for the company and quite capable of reaching great heights. This makes the criticism seem less personal as it assesses the work. The feedback given to the team member is immediate and is impactful. Employees tend to correct their mistakes as soon as the message is conveyed to them.

How to Praise Intentionally

A leader knows exactly when to praise and when to criticize. Gino and Wickman, in their book, "How to Be a Great Boss" describe the four types of leaders: those who do not know how to praise or criticize, and those who consciously use criticism and praise (North, 2019). According to the authors, a "cheerleader" is one who uses excessive praise. The problem with this approach is that it may lead to mediocrity and poor morale among the employees. They then describe the "poor boss" who does not provide proper feedback, leaving what is called a "feedback vacuum" and leaves employees wondering what to expect. This approach leaves the employees unsatisfied with their jobs and their boss. Then comes the "taskmaster", who provides feedback, but is never quite good at praising people for a job well done. This creates a "praise vacuum", giving employees the impression that getting praise is something extremely hard to come by. Such an attitude can adversely affect their performance. The authors finally describe the "great boss" who is good at giving authentic feedback in the form of criticism as well as praise. Such leaders are great at developing high-performing teams, fostering accountability, and promoting high standards in the organizational culture.

Publicly praising and recognizing the contribution of employees is quite meaningful in terms of encouraging and raising the morale of the one being praised as well as helping the other team members learn something new. Publicly praising the employee must be done in an elaborate manner (Scott, n.d.-a). The work done by the employee, the context that it had, as well as the overall impact of his or her contribution must be clearly stated. Also, state how the peers and the organization benefited from the contribution of the employee. While public praise works well in the majority of the cases, there may be exceptions to the rule, and some individuals may not feel comfortable being praised publicly. It's best to assume a personalized approach to achieve the best results while delivering feedback. Finally, following up public praise with an email reinforces it and shows an attitude of caring and compassion.

On the whole, consistent feedback must be a learning experience for all employees. Furthermore, a good boss allows his or her team to criticize their leadership and management skills in public as it gives them a chance to correct their attitude and behavior, or explain their stance to the team in a transparent manner. Iarocci (2018) indicates that servant leaders use more praise and less criticism to be effective. The strategy proves valuable as we are wired to see negative aspects more frequently than positive ones. Criticism seems to have a more profound impact on the individual when compared to praise. Even when criticism is used in a situation when a warning is highly essential, it undermines the confidence of an individual and does not inspire them to put their best foot forward. On the converse side, positive feedback is highly motivational and promotes creativity.

Chapter Summary

- Feedback must be clear, immediate, and in-person. Criticism should be done in private and about what went wrong, and not criticize the person who made the mistake.
- One-minute goals help understand needs, measure performance, and check progress to identify if results have been achieved.
- An ideal ratio for praise:criticism is 5:1, which can be achieved by identifying opportunities, praising in a timely manner, and addressing problems.
- When negative feedback is constructive and based on the expertise of the person and a relevant scale, it leads to motivation, success, and improved performance.
- Public criticism makes people feel humiliated, embarrassed, resentful, and unmotivated. Leaders must only use public criticism to prevent illegal or abusive behavior.
- Private criticism that is immediate and clear improves performance.
- Public and intentional praise raises employee morale, creativity, and motivation when it is elaborate, compassionate, and consistent.

Chapter Six: Leading Through Change

Something unexpected is about to happen! David is going to lead the organization to a transition to Infrastructure as a Service (IaaS). He's unsure at first - he wonders whether Goliath will be there to support him through this. He approaches Goliath with an empathetic attitude, and experiences the most unexpected change - not just in the IT wing but also in Goliath's attitude …

To Lead through Change means to Share Goals, have a Plan, and follow-through Gradually

David has a great goal – to move the organization to Infrastructure as a Service (IaaS). He decides to go for the hybrid cloud model. He has goals and deadlines, a plan, and roadmap.
"It's an ambitious project, but with the support I will get from Alice, John, Oliver, Sophia, and Goliath, I can already imagine things falling in place."
"… and Goliath," he mulls.

[In Goliath's office]
"Hello there, Goliath," greets David with a smile. He takes a step forward to shake hands with Goliath when he realizes his foot is in a coffee pool. David shifts his gaze from Goliath to the coffee mess on the floor. David gets it instantly. Goliath is anxious about the change!

As if unaffected by the coffee mishap, David continues to offer his hand, reaching out to Goliath warmly. Goliath is moved by David's supportive attitude as he admits the numerous instances of impolite cold-hearted exchanges he had with David in the past. Goliath is impressed by David's empathy and decides to be a different person this time.

It is Critical to Manage Expectations Well and Communicate Effectively during Change

David: Hello team! Here's the agenda to move to IaaS. Please have a copy for yourself and pass the rest. Attached to the agenda is a list of answers to your common questions. When you have read it, you will know who does what, how moving to IaaS will affect you, and how Goliath and I will help you.

Goliath: Team, it's great to hear about the new move from David. Do keep in mind that I'll be there to provide feedback, updates, and clarify your roles. You can count on me!

Alice: Sure we will, Goliath. You make it sound like a breeze!
[cheers from the team]

[After five days]
Goliath: That was quick. Great momentum from the team! Remember to keep in touch for the weekly performance assessment. We are bound to capture the market effortlessly!

Change is a constant process, sometimes related to the reorganization of a department and at other times about retaining talent. Even when change is happening all the time, most employees associate it with fear as there is a certain uncertainty involved.

Leadership in the face of change is a difficult process. They may be anxious about the unknown and a few effective strategies can make change management a successful process (Sturt & Nordstrom, 2016).

- <u>Share Information</u>: As a leader, change management may seem to be intimidating. You can make things simpler by involving your team in the important details including the broad goals, deadlines, and other important information. Sharing information with the team helps overcome worries and also empowers the team.
- <u>Have a Good Plan</u>: When you know what you need, it is time to make a plan. Let each of your team members know their duties according to their competencies and skills. Moving beyond sharing a vision, and being specific about the plan with input from the team members allows them to contribute their ideas and take ownership of the situation. It also boosts their confidence.
- <u>Listen to Questions and Address Them</u>: Listen to the concerns of your team members as well as any questions they may have. Allow time for sharing their opinion and assist them in sorting out their concerns. Help them understand your commitment towards the cause by explaining to them that you are available to assist them. Inquiring specifically if you can help them in any way engages them for a smooth transition.
- <u>Deal with Change Gradually</u>: It is best to imbibe change gradually. When change is embraced suddenly, it may become overwhelming for your team and disrupt the daily schedule. Change requires a restructuring of the workspace and new roles for employees. Incorporating change gradually helps the team understand how they can embrace change for their advantage.

- <u>Appreciate Good Performance</u>: While change management comes with a lot of challenges, leaders must always be mindful of appreciating the team for their good performance. It is important for leaders to find time to appreciate their team and make them feel valuable throughout the change management process. To be successful in doing this, leaders must set time separately to have a clear reflection of the team performance, and set time to appreciate them.
- <u>Manage Conflicts Effectively</u>: Conflicts are inevitable in change management. The primary reasons for conflict during change management relate to inadequate information about the roles of team members, or an unusual response to the pace of change. Effective leaders must be able to resolve conflict constructively by addressing mistakes and miscommunications and targeting constructive solutions.

Empathy in Change Management

Understanding the emotional and psychological states of employees is important for leaders to counter challenges, set priorities, and manage the team. Understand the anxiety and uncertainty that the team may be going through, and extend the right type of support to everyone involved. To be an effective leader, it is important to understand emotions and support employees. Finally, help your team cope with uncertainty and make adjustments (Blue Beyond Consulting, 2020). The change process is associated with feelings of loss as certain things will no longer continue to exist in the new scenario. The process of transition which features the creation of new roles and processes is accompanied by confusion, which leads to new beginnings with new understandings and new values. This "emotional process of change" can be a strategic way to lead employees into the new world through empathy and encouragement:

- When the employees begin to feel a sense of loss for what will be left behind, be empathetic, acknowledge their feelings, create a safe sharing space, clearly specify expectations, and communicate at a personal level.
- During the transition phase, find ways to help the team adapt, engage them to create solutions together, set expectations to facilitate progress, and communicate frequently with the team.
- When the team starts to adapt to the new model, ensure that the desired processes and systems are in place, encourage the team, reward them for their accomplishments, and make the required adjustments needed for the new system to work as expected.

Managing the Expectations of People

Planning is an important aspect of change management. Change in the positive direction entails a good understanding of the feelings, thoughts, and expectations of the team. Most change initiatives fail when the concerns of employees are not addressed and they are only minimally involved in the process (Ruhmann, 2020). Effective leaders must be able to address at least these five concerns pertaining to the change management process:

- Employees often want to know why the change is required and what will be affected by the change (information concerns).
- They will want to know who will be able to help them through the change process and whether the change is realistic (implementation concerns).
- On an individual level, employees may want to know how the change will affect them and if it is possible for them to learn to bring about the change (personal concerns).

- Employees may be curious if they can trust their leaders and rely on their guidance through the change process (refinement concerns).
- The team may want to evaluate if the change is worthy of their effort and whether it will work for all of them (impact concerns).

Communication In Times of Change

Communication is very important in times of change as it creates an environment that promotes a sense of safety for changing the mindsets of employees. Leaders who are good communicators provide their employees with the right set of tools to facilitate a positive shift in their attitudes for a sustainable transformation (Gaskell, 2019). When guiding your organization towards change, follow these best practices (Wood, 2019):

- Communicate ahead of time so that employees do not misinterpret the upcoming change. Leaders are in charge of "setting the tone and content".
- Change requires building connections based on trust. Leaders must live up to their promises to retain trust from existing and new connections.
- Repeat messages that are meaningful to help employees imbibe the message well.
- Visibility is a key aspect of effective leadership. Leading with confidence and "being there" is important to manage change effectively.
- Inform employees about the impact of the change, and the way in which it affects their roles and jobs.
- Appreciate employees for their small or big successes to allay the anxieties of your employees and build momentum.
- Build strategies for two-way communication, and introduce communication tools such as feedback loops, meetings, and

the like, to ensure messages are exchanged in both directions.
- Develop a single standard to communicate your mission, vision, values, and strategy and ensure all members of the team communicate this information in a consistent manner.
- Share your vision with your employees and then break down the next steps into achievable tasks to keep the team focused and maintain their momentum.
- Even when there is a course of action, taking on a new direction requires trust, communication, and support from employees, and they may even require guidance to make the necessary corrections along the course.

Effective Strategies for COVID-19

Bruce (2020) indicates that COVID-19 has increased anxiety, depression, and workplace burnout, and its associated costs are estimated to be $125 billion annually. Burnout can surface as physical as well as emotional exhaustion, which can result in detachment and "feeling of being ineffective". The pandemic is linked to change, uncertainty, and grief, and employees are required to possess a high level of resilience and adaptability (Bruce, 2020). Resilient and adaptable employees seem to be more agile (28%) and less prone to depression and anxiety (only 2% or less). Moreover, leaders must be able to build cognitive skills and provide the necessary resources to alleviate "change fatigue", which is a situation that arises when the responsibilities imposed on employees exceed the resources provided to them.

The COVID-19 pandemic has put employees at risk of mental and emotional health challenges, and the nature of the response from leaders can make a difference to employees and the organization (Greenberg, 2020). This time of crisis requires leaders to make their team more resilient and be able to connect by assuming a compassionate approach. Leaders must be able to cultivate skills for crisis response in their employees. The authors uphold the importance of "self-leadership" which is essential to be able to lead others effectively:

- Recognizing your own emotions are very important as you avoid projecting them onto others. A popular technique in psychology to track your own emotions is to imagine a thermometer with the lower part depicting cool temperatures and the upper part depicting hot temperatures. This is a representation of your "emotional temperature" and helps you take control of your feelings
- Setting goals is critical to functioning successfully in a crisis. Leaders often over-function by setting goals they cannot achieve, or under-function by losing hope when they imagine the crisis as something invincible, often giving up hope sooner rather than later. The best way to move forward is to set realistic goals by making an assessment of your goals by consulting a trusted person or coach.
- Leaders must set time aside to promote their emotional health intentionally by engaging in relevant activities such as exercising regularly or having a restful sleep.
- Practice the technique of radical acceptance that entails accepting reality and minimizing negative feelings about thinking about what should have been the situation. When you feel you are not in sync with reality, a good recommended practice is to breathe in while accepting curiosity and then breathing out while you let go of your judgment.
- It is important to look at the positive side and feel happy about it. Successful leaders develop a positive attitude even in trying circumstances by enjoying the little things in life such as not having to commute to the office. Positivity and gratitude go a long way to foster well-being.

The COVID-19 crisis requires leaders to ensure the wellbeing of their employees through an attitude of compassion. The stress experienced during the coronavirus epidemic has made most risk mitigation strategies and contingency plans ineffective. According to reliable research evidence, employees in any organization need stability, hope, trust, and compassion. In these trying circumstances, it is important to follow specific strategies when leading your employees (Ratanjee & Gandhi, 2020):

- <u>Leadership Presence</u>: Ratanjee and Gandhi (2020) draw upon the insights of Gallup research and indicate that strategies must be tailored towards remote work through the values of compassion and care when communicating with employees through videos. Leaders can enforce their vision and values by sending messages of "optimism and hope" to key stakeholders during this challenging situation. Video communication is important as departments have different roles, and employees and managers are involved in different types of operations. When managers and employees witness your presence, they are more likely to participate in conversations to enhance performance for their success.
- <u>Give Hope</u>: Many companies have executed their unique strategies in the face of the COVID-19 crisis, to make a unique contribution towards the pandemic response. Contributions from leading market players, such as delivering medical equipment and hand sanitizers free of charge help save lives, build a better future, and serve as an inspiration for the other employees. In the face of the COVID-19 crisis, frequently communicate your purpose and values to your employees, and help them imbibe them. Even when your organization is not able to make material contributions, care, compassion, and empathy go a long way in helping and boosting the morale of customers and employees.

- <u>Provide Stability</u>: The COVID-19 crisis has exerted extreme stress on the wellbeing of people in different dimensions including social, financial, and career. As many as 72% of the people feel that they will be affected by the coronavirus and 52% feel that they will face a financial crisis. Employees may also face a major setback from "emotional exhaustion", which may adversely influence their performance. Effective leadership means you are able to understand the impact of these elements and have the necessary strategies in place to counteract the adverse effects. When change is initiated, not everything may fall in place as expected (Wolf, 2020). Leaders must be prepared to face all types of challenges by being calm and positive.
- <u>Involve your Team</u>: Accepting input from your teammates makes them feel valued. When communicating with your team, ensure that you practice clarity and are specific about what you want to communicate. An overworked system is hard to cope with, and it becomes difficult to focus on complex goals. Communicating clearly what kind of support you can offer your team is critical to success. Secondly, when working with your team, accept that they are not able to put their best foot forward and adjust goals accordingly (Greenberg, 2020). Finally, leaders must invest resources to support the mental health concerns of their employees and promote the well-being of the workers. Resources may also be allocated to cope with trying times when team members may fall sick, lose their loved ones, or may have to deal with other family issues.

Chapter Summary

- Change is constant but associated with uncertainty.
- Change can be managed with effective strategies such as sharing information (intimidating but empowering), planning well (take ownership and boost confidence), address queries (understand concerns and engage team), enforce change gradually (understand how to embrace change), appreciate performance (reflect clearly and praise), and manage conflict (resolve constructively and address miscommunication).
- Empathy in change management requires leaders to understand the psychological and emotional states of employees.
- Empathy means understanding uncertainty and anxiety, adjusting to the situation, and encouraging a smooth transition.
- Change management requires planning, which requires knowing the reason for the change, who will help with the process, the effects of change, the trustworthiness of leaders, and plausibility of the change.
- Communication during change promotes communicating proactively, building connections, repeating meaningful messages, appreciating employees, promoting two-way communication, maintaining visibility, informing about the impact of change, sharing the vision, and giving a new direction.
- Change during the COVID-19 era requires recognizing emotions, setting goals, promoting emotional health, practicing radical acceptance, and staying positive.

The Power Of Intentional Leadership

Chapter Seven: The Art Of Duck Leadership

Goliath identifies him well with the team and wishes to be part of the exciting new plan. David is leading impeccably well, with his duck leadership style. There has never been a time with greater harmony and happiness all around. Goliath now understands the value of team bonding and how resilience can pull them through every adversity. He chooses to "be there" and alleviate concerns that David may have from this tough job in the future. As it is rightly said, the V-formation of birds is one of the most delightful sights, and the team is going to experience bonding and empowerment like never before …

Duck Leadership

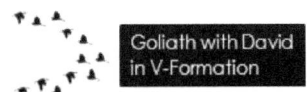

Goliath with David in V-Formation

Leaders can Learn Many Things from Birds – Organization, Resilience, Effort, Composure, and Leading by Example …

David always looks for new ways to engage his team, so that work is fun. He believes that good bonding can produce exceptional results. It's the big day for David with another great quarter and 100% satisfied customers. David is going to meet his team for their next big phase of business development. There's a lot on David's checklist – who is to liaise with the customers, how will they deliver services, who is going to oversee the support staff for smooth after-sales services, who will sign agreements, and a lot many aspects of service delivery.

David: Oh Hello Goliath! You are here before everyone else! It's great to see you.
Goliath: Pleasure is all mine, David. I see that you are looking at giving us new sales targets and new responsibilities for an exciting quarter. I am really looking forward to all the excitement. Our new service portfolio is a cut above the rest, David.
David: It sure is! We have everything that the customers demanded in their last feedback. We should have a bunch of happy faces this time…

[Alice, John, Sophia, and Oliver arrive. All team members greet each other]

David: I am going to briefly describe how we plan to approach business development this time. Our strategy is a bit different when compared to the last quarter. We have a better budget, and that's a big plus. We also have a bigger team, and that means more hard work and more customers. I am leading you all for a while, but we will need to switch roles, to be a resilient team and keep ourselves from getting stressed. Here's a copy of my notes. It's a collection of my thoughts, but we can update that with your help.

Being Like Birds Teaches Perseverance, Engagement, Trust, Empowerment, and Much More …

[Agreement. Team disperses but Goliath stays for a while]

Goliath: [Pointing at David's notes] David, this is a clever plan. I never guessed you would include social media in our marketing campaign. It's going to be a blockbuster with the COVID pairing man and machine!
[David gives Goliath a broad smile]

Goliath: Looks like a tough job. I will be there for you and be the leading duck in the V-formation when you feel like flapping your wings a little less harder.
[David smiles ear-to-ear]

Ducks are wonderful creatures and can teach a lot about effective leadership. Feeding the ducks at the pond leads to many unexpected observations that we can apply to obtain success as a leader. To understand what ducks can teach you, let's recollect what it is like to see a duck waddling in the pond along with her ducklings (Rosenberg, 2012; Fiore, 2016):

Ducks Lead Their Young With Their Unique Style

Ducklings follow their mother duck in a specific formation, most often the V formation when they fly. The mama duck always leads the other ducklings to take them to the destination. What they accomplish at the end of the journey relates to the joint effort of the duck and its ducklings. If the ducklings did not follow the duck or the duck did not lead them, they would not be able to reach their destination (Rosenberg, 2012).

<u>Leadership Qualities</u>

Leaders should also lead their team to success by setting an example for them to follow. They must display important qualities that are expected from successful leaders. They must encourage teamwork and lead by example. Experts believe that when leaders set an example to lead their team, they are also successful in building a succession plan for their followers (Rosenberg, 2012).

Ducks Have Distinct Roles Within Their Team

Ducks often take up their duties, and it's amazing how they act them out in perfect harmony and synchronization. If you have observed the flock carefully and closely, you must have most likely spotted the watch duck who keeps an eye on the bushes for any possible unexpected movements as they may signal the presence of a predator. These ducks take a position at the end of the line when going waddling in the pool or looking for food. They communicate possible danger by quacking loudly. The youngest duck is often spotted watching for predators just before going to bed, to let the group know that there is a predator in the vicinity (McBride, 2015).

Leadership Organization

Similar to birds, leaders are successful when they organize their team so the members have different roles to play, and have clarity on their purpose. Successful leaders are able to break down tasks into subunits the team can work with to achieve success with the broad goal. Leaders communicate their vision and when the team believes in the vision of the leader, they are able to execute the tasks assigned in a way that they are able to meet expectations. This eventually leads to the success of the team (McBride, 2015)

Ducks Let Water Roll Off Their Back

The waterproof feathers of ducks do not let water stick to them for long when they are splashed. Beads of water form on the back of ducks, and the water rolls back into the pond after a while or sometimes with some effort to take it off their backs (Poke, 2011).

Leadership Resilience

This character may be compared to the resilience expected from leaders. The beads of water that momentarily get on the duck's back may be compared to problems that may pop up now and then for a leader. A determined leader keeps his or her attention on the vision and goal and abstains from dwelling in problems for too long. He or she displays resilience and "dust off" minor distractions while staying focused on the broad goals. This attitude is also useful in deflecting major obstacles as they come in the way of leaders (Poke, 2011; Rosenberg, 2012).

Ducks Are Tranquil On the Surface, Even When They Are Working Hard

Ducks always appear to be waddling peacefully when you watch them from a distance. Although it may look like they are expending very little effort to waddle on the waters, they are applying great effort under the surface of the water to move forward. Ducks do this in a frantic effort to keep themselves afloat (Poke, 2011; Rosenberg, 2012).

<u>Leadership Composure</u>

The calm waddling of the ducks as it appears may be compared to the composure a leader must display at all times while leading his or her team. Sometimes, leaders may make it obvious how stressed and worn out they are feeling after a hard day's work. However, this is not the ideal thing to do. Instead, it makes more sense to display calmness so that the team does not reflect the agitation of the leader. Being calm and composed while working hard on high-priority tasks and solving problems and distractions makes the team members perceive the leader as someone the team can trust and rely on for assistance, especially when there is a crisis situation (Poke, 2011; Rosenberg, 2012).

Ducks Put Their Head In the Water to Get Food

Ducks have to put their head down to look for food and grab it. Unless they make that effort, it is not possible to find the food that is important for their survival. They do not depend on someone else to find food for them and undertake all that it takes to go down into the water while holding their breath, to find the kind of prey they are looking for (Poke, 2011).

Leadership Effort

Leaders need to put a similar kind of effort to accomplish certain tasks that need their personal attention. Leaders can delegate tasks when they feel appropriate, but there are many decisions they have to take on their own. Leadership is associated with great responsibility, and leaders must be willing to take full control when the situation demands it. Many critical tasks require dedicated attention from leaders, and the right degree of effort expended by a leader helps to achieve great improvements in performance (Poke, 2011).

Ducklings Follow the First Thing They See

When an egg cracks and the duckling pops its head out to witness the world outside, it follows the first thing that it sees. This behavior is known as imprinting and is exhibited by the duckling even when it does not see the mother duck. It follows whoever it sees. It may follow a dog, or it may even follow another person (Poke, 2011).

Leadership Example

Leaders must set examples for their followers to imbibe. If their followers do not find them as often as they expect, or do not see them as role models, they are more likely to follow someone else. To ensure that leaders have a good followership, they should provide a sound vision and deliver that vision. They must also deliver consistent messages to their followers to prevent distractions. This behavior helps them to establish a regular focus on the task. It also helps to prevent unwanted influence, such as from a negative person from working its way to your team members and steering them into something completely unnecessary (Poke, 2011).

Beyond imbibing the basic traits of ducks and ducklings, there are several lessons leaders can learn from the way ducks communicate, form a community, and face challenges:

- <u>Persevere in Adversity</u>: Ducks never give up even in the most difficult of times. Duck leadership is, in part, about perseverance in the face of adversity (Lu, 2014).
- <u>Keep the Team Together</u>: Ducks always do things together. They quack together, fly together, east together, and swim together. Keeping the team together helps leaders maintain a high level of motivation with little effort. Leaders must make sure they keep the whole team engaged and everyone gets to participate and feel a high sense of self-worth (Lu, 2014).
- <u>Focus on Your Goal to Gain Momentum</u>: Geese fly in the V-formation to achieve momentum and get to the destination faster and with less energy expended during their flight. The flapping of the wings in a synchronized manner causes an uplift that reduces the friction in the air and achieves a 70% increase in the flying range. Leaders can imbibe this trait to lead their team towards a common goal, by gaining enough momentum through teamwork and collective action (Palizban, 2012).
- <u>Foster Commitment for a Shared Purpose</u>: When geese migrate, they take the same route every year. The members of the flock may change, but the route never changes. Parents teach their children what route they must take to fly to their destination (Palizban, 2012). Leaders can imbibe the essential character of commitment from this attitude of the geese. Leaders must help their team understand core values and the purpose of the organization, and encourage them to stay committed to it. The core values and purpose never change, even though the means to achieve it undergo significant improvements. Leaders may apply different strategies to achieve the purpose, but their team must

understand how important it is to stay committed to the purpose.

- <u>Trust your Team</u>: The mother duck does not always tell her ducklings what to do. Sometimes, they try their techniques when learning to fly. Leaders must be willing to trust their team to complete a task their way even when the team is less qualified or experienced (Lu, 2014).
- <u>Be open to Changing Roles</u>: Geese are graceful enough to change their roles when the need arises. Sometimes, when the goose in front is tired of flying, it may get back to a place far back in the formation, allowing another goose to lead the flight. In this way, they cooperate and exchange leadership positions, and in the bargain maintain a swift and continuous flight to reach their destination in the shortest possible time (Palizban, 2012). Leaders who are successful empower others to lead. Too much control in the hands of a leader tends to burn him or her out. Control also reduces motivation and employees do not feel like engaging in the activity for long. However, understanding the unique capabilities, gifts, and skills of employees empowers them and allows them to show off their unique talents. Giving the team members a chance to lead results in unexpected outcomes.
- <u>Increase Visibility</u>: When geese fly in a V-formation, they are able to see what is happening in front of them, and their view is not really blocked by the other geese, or other distractions and obstacles. Geese teach leaders that visibility is extremely important for organizational success. Organizations must possess both top-down as well as bottom-up visibility. Top-down visibility is meant for the leaders as they can have a good view of what is going on in an organization and make good decisions. Bottom-up visibility allows employees to engage in the activities of the organization, and have a good view of the "bigger picture". Having enough information gives the team a sense of

empowerment and they feel valued about making contributions (Palizban, 2012).

- Face Challenges, not Avoid Them: Ducklings are conditioned to either go over an obstacle when they encounter it or pass through it. They never try to avoid obstacles and face challenges head-on. Leaders who lead by example teach their team to face the challenge and find a way through it as there is sometimes no other way of getting around the challenge (Lu, 2014).
- Offer Support When Things Get Out of Control: An important aspect of teamwork among the geese is that sick geese are never left to carry on by themselves. When a goose is sick, two other geese drop out of the formation to follow the goose down and offer the required protection. They are faithful companions and never leave the sick goose. They wait until it is fit enough to fly or accompany it until it dies. Once the matter is resolved, they join their old flock or form a new formation and move forward (Palizban, 2012). Leaders can learn a lot from this quality of the geese. They can teach their team to develop an attitude of faithfulness towards each other, especially when they face difficult times. Teams are often found to stay together when everything is going fine. However, they tend to fall apart in the face of difficulty. team members must realize that they need each other most when there are challenges and team bonding is essential to support a member when he or she needs help.
- Seek Help When you Have To: Leaders must teach all members of their team to seek help when they have to, just like the geese in the V formation. When a goose accidentally falls out of the formation when flying, it quickly comes back so that it is aligned with the goose in front of it. This allows it to take advantage of the lift created by the bird in front of it. In line with this analogy, it is important to understand that no matter how capable and experienced a leader or an

employee is, there may be times when they need help to successfully overcome a certain challenge (Palizban, 2012).
- <u>Acknowledge Good Performance</u>: When a goose does something extraordinary, the other geese honk to provide due recognition and encourage it to move on with greater motivation and speed (Palizban, 2012). Praising is an important aspect of effective leadership. Appreciating someone for their good work inspires them to do even better next time. It is the way to make them feel valued and respected. When an employee puts his or her heart and soul to accomplish something great, and there is no feedback from the leader acknowledging his or her outstanding contribution, the employee may feel dissatisfied. Sometimes, bad leadership and the tendency to take everything for granted may lead the employee into quitting their job. Noticing employees and encouraging them helps to keep the team motivated and achieve their goals.

Chapter Summary

- Leaders can learn a lot from ducks from their manners of feeding the young, waddling in the pond, and flying in V-formation.
- Ducks teach you to set an example for your followers.
- Leaders can organize their team to have a clear purpose and different roles.
- Ducks teach resilience from the way they roll off water from their feathers back into the pond.
- Leaders can learn to display composure in adversity by looking at the way ducks waddle - peacefully on the top and great effort under the water surface.
- Sometimes leaders need to put in extra effort and personal attention for important tasks, just like ducks that put their head under the water to reach for food.

- Leaders must be visible for their followers to imbibe their example.
- Leaders can gain a good understanding of several important leadership traits from ducks, such as perseverance, focus, unity, trust, and commitment.
- Finally, ducks teach how to face challenges, stay visible to the team, offer support, get help, be prepared to switch roles, and recognize good performance.

Chapter Eight: Patience, Flexibility, & Adaptability

Goliath reflects on how much he achieved in so little time with a change in his mindset. David made him realize his full potential, and he counts his blessings. Goliath is a major contributor to the company's growth and the figures say it all. People want him more than anyone else, and he earned it with his hard work and David's intentional leadership …

Patience, Flexibility, and Adaptability

Goliath Becomes a Trailblazer

Goliath is ever so grateful to David for his empathy that led to a great transformation within him. He cannot thank him enough for all the support he has from the team now. Everything seems to fall in place. It's as if he always belonged to the team, and he had wrongly assumed that he would never be able to "fit in".

Patience Leads to Success and Impatience Leads to Financial Trouble

Goliath reflects on how much achieved along his journey with David: he does not lose temper anymore, there were no major losses, he's so much more productive, he's smiling always, he's not short on time anymore, customers like his suggestions, and above all, he commands respect.

[Goliath and David meet in the lounge over a cup of coffee. They happen to have all the time. IT automation makes it possible to have more human contact. It's their helping hand after the recent technology upgrade]

Goliath: David, you have been a great mentor. You never even made me feel I lacked somewhere. I have come a long way, and with high profile customers like CloudStrike and MegaBusiness choosing us year after year, I feel so blessed. The credit goes to you, David.

David: That's being very generous, Goliath. You had a lot of untapped potential. I just helped you see that from a different perspective. You are a star and the company needs performers like you. Remember the cloud migration for ElectecHealth. Their data stores were huge, and getting even a small record would take forever. You did the big thinking and chose the patient at the core of the information design. That hit the target and they slashed data storage cost by 83%. You did great by moving the physical infrastructure too. They got 100 more beds, and they don't even worry about having more data. The system takes care of it.

Flexibility and Adaptability Leads to Good Decisions

Goliath: It was a never-before experience. It was at ElectecHealth that I ran into Mike, who offered me a role at his charity organization. He said he liked to have someone adaptable to work with the stakeholders, and spontaneously decide where the charity money goes. He said, "You are the one who can understand people from their body language, and I have not seen many like that before."

David: Oh, that's a wonderful opportunity. Go for it, Goliath. The people will welcome you warmly.

Goliath: Thanks for everything, David. You're the best.

Leadership Patience

Patience has been perceived in different ways over the years. It is often regarded as something "difficult to practice", the ability to wait, or putting up with difficulties. Leaders may often go through a degree of impatience that is proportional to the magnitude of the crisis. However, composure is often associated with patience and is essential to realize long-term goals. Leaders may not always be able to practice patience as the environment is conditioned to demand quick decisions from them. However, patience allows them to assess the situation and the right strategy and resources for an effective outcome (Moran, 2010). History is witness to the role of patience in leadership successes such as in the case of Benjamin Franklin's contribution to American independence and Mahatma Gandhi's efforts to free India from British rule.

On the converse side, impatience is often associated with financial trouble. The international financial crisis demonstrates this idea as the basis of the problem is deeply rooted in the impatient attitude of the consumers, regulators. lenders, investors, and other stakeholders. The desire to achieve immediate results often leads to adverse outcomes (Moran, 2010). Leading with patience requires a good understanding of the situation and an analysis of the skills needed. Patience is also important while creating an effective plan to move forward with the support and confidence of key stakeholders. While pursuing your goal, patience is highly desirable to engage stakeholders and retain their support. As you build confidence, you will be able to meet your goals and effectively respond to unexpected events.

Patience is an important aspect of the workplace environment as it provides the fabric to enable the team to take on calculated risks or engage in healthy conflict. A patient leader displays self-control and commands authority. The virtue of patience is apparent in all aspects, from strategy to relationships, and the leader becomes the role model, being able to face difficulties without getting frustrated (Harmon, 2014). As a result, the patient leader is able to gain a higher degree of engagement and commitment.

Patience is a very important aspect of leadership success. Experts believe that there may be several ways to learn to be patient based on one's experiences, and that patience is an important aspect of leadership. There are several reasons why you may want to practice patience as a leader. A few aspects are explained below (Todorovic, 2019):

- <u>Being Patient Helps you Get Respect</u>: Team members take time to trust and respect you as a leader. During this period, you must exercise patience and let the team feel comfortable. Being patient and gaining respect fosters commitment that is essential in the long run. Patience causes you to differentiate yourself and gain a positive reputation in the long run.
- <u>Being Patient Helps Team Members Progress</u>: Team members are always looking for opportunities to make progress. They have different skills and process information in different ways. Being patient as a leader allows them the time and freedom to improve and make a mark. In doing so, you also gain trust from the team. Patience inculcates persistence and commitment and helps teams grow.
- <u>Being Patient Improves Productivity</u>: Team members have their own style and pace of working. Exercising patience as a leader gives them freedom and space to work through the task by putting their best foot forward. Leaders who are patient act as catalysts to realize productivity in the short term as well as the long run. Leaders who are patient also allow team members to take breaks and the much-needed rest when they require it the most. This is an essential aspect of staying on track and staying motivated and productive.
- <u>Being Patient Fosters Positive Attitude</u>: Leaders who are patient when faced with challenges become role models for

their team as they take the necessary action while projecting a positive attitude. Leaders are able to transfer this positivity to their team members and organization and motivate them for organizational success.

- <u>Being Patient Improves Time Management</u>: Leaders are often faced with a multitude of responsibilities and may sometimes overburden their team beyond their limits to be able to meet their goals in time. However, this approach is far from efficient and may become the reason for dissatisfaction among employees. Leaders can apply patience to improve their time management skills and increase efficiency.
- <u>Being Patient Helps Make Good Decisions for Success</u>: Decision-making is an essential aspect of leadership. When a leader has patience while making decisions, he or she is able to avoid influencing the team and the organization negatively. Taking some time and making decisions patiently is far better than instantaneous decisions that hurt the team. Over time, leaders can achieve great results through good decision-making and develop a positive company culture.
- <u>Being Patient Helps Adapt to Change</u>: When leaders practice patience, they are able to adapt to change easily. Change is perceived by the different team members in different ways. Some team members may imbibe the change easily, while others may find it sudden and take more time to adapt to the change. Leaders must understand the unique needs of their team members and be patient with those who require more time to adapt to the change.

In essence, patience is a virtue and art that may be adapted gradually when there is a willingness to do so. When perceived in a simple way, patience is about asking questions and waiting to get answers to make the right decisions. In being patient, you trade urgency for insight, judgment, and creativity, and project a positive attitude and composed appearance. Although patience is tested quite often, it is an important aspect of the overall well-being of the team and fosters productivity (*Patience and Leadership in Our Current World*, 2021). Impatience happens when our goals become difficult to achieve in terms of time or effort required. Impatience associated with a specific task can have ripple effects and influence our relationships with colleagues and family.

You can improve your patience by increasing self-awareness to recognize warning signs in terms of the clues your body provides, and use techniques such as mindfulness to proactively deal with destructive thoughts and behaviors (*Patience and Leadership in Our Current World*, 2021). Some of the positive strategies that lead to a greater degree of patience include accepting control to the extent that is possible, being kind, positive, and balanced, adjusting expectations so they are more realistic, prioritizing duties, and engaging in self-reflection. Patient leaders are empowered and compassionate and are able to build confidence and trust within teams.

Flexibility and Adaptability

Practicing Flexibility for Strong Leadership

Continuous skill development is an important aspect of success with personal development and leadership growth. Flexibility is an important element in this context when uncertainty demands constant adaptability to survive in a changing environment (Haggerty, 2020). Effective leadership can be developed by applying flexibility in the following ways:

- Flexibility and positive change depend on the cooperation between team members. Being an effective leader does not just mean proposing and implementing great ideas, but it also means being able to acknowledge the ideas of your colleagues. Sometimes, leaders tend to impulsively reject the ideas of their colleagues, but when you ask questions with an intent to apply the idea, the outcome is much different and it also helps to build trust and a deeper connection with your coworkers.

- Sometimes, opportunities may bring great rewards for your business, but may also require additional flexibility and the need to develop a product that does not belong to your original portfolio. Resisting the change that defines the success of this project may mean doing away with the opportunity. The best thing to do in this scenario is to embrace innovation and be one of the early adopters.
- Staying flexible and getting to new heights by making good decisions requires making changes to the daily routine. You may want to make changes to simple things such as commuting to the office, having a different morning routine, and gaining renewed energy for inspiration.
- Experts believe that it is possible to bring about positive change in the work environment by applying "rebel leadership", which involves breaking rules to tap into new ideas. Rebellion in the workplace has a positive aspect to it since it creates harmony in the personal and professional lives of employees. There are several areas to bring about positive change including processes and protocols implemented in the workplace.
- Leaders may not always be able to make a difference by "setting the tone" for meetings. The desired change may come when a leader is able to adapt to the people they work with. Communicating and inviting the viewpoints of others leads to productivity. Furthermore, flexibility also refers to anticipating and making changes to your direction to be able to utilize your energy in a positive manner.

Different Leadership Styles for Flexibility in Organizations

Leaders need to apply different styles to be effective and achieve success.

- A leader who is an idol is one who is able to lead by example. An icon leader has a strong presence and is able to convince his or her followers to meet the set standards. However, this style may not be suitable for everyone as it is associated with someone who can inspire others.
- A leader may function as a coach that has considerable authority attached to it. The leader can be either encouraging, suggesting to the team what is best for them, or assuming a more commanding tone to get things done.
- Some leaders are macromanagers and focus on the bigger picture. Macromanagers tend to assume the responsibility of big tasks and delegate other tasks to their employees.
- On the other hand, micromanagers try to control every aspect of business processes. They are focused on a single vision and engage their employees to execute tasks that help to achieve their vision. However, this style of leadership may make most employees unhappy.
- A beloved leader is one who can get people to follow his or her advice and lead them to a better environment. Beloved leaders have considerable charisma and charm.
- Leaders can be adapters who are able to adjust to any type of environment. They learn a variety of different skills and apply them to their different roles. They do not limit themselves to a single role and are focused on several different roles, which they execute competently.
- A trailblazer is a leader with a different perspective, and the strategies are often unique. Their unconventional thinking often leads to surprising outcomes.

- A revolutionary leader discovers even more than a trailblazer and can assume new and creative techniques and break new ground.

Applying Situational Leadership to Engage Employees for Productive Organizations

Situational leadership is an adaptive style of leadership related to the development behavior of employees. Situational leadership refers to the ability of a leader to look at situations from several perspectives (*Situational Leadership and How Flexibility Leads to Success*, 2019). Situational leaders can also work as progressive leaders (lead by example and have high expectations from followers), authoritative leaders (identifying challenges and analyzing problems), and coaching leaders (individual's skills on job and their personal development). To be an effective leader, you need to make a fair assessment of the situation and the employee behavior to apply the right leadership approach. In effect, today's complex business environments require you to apply situational leadership skills to achieve success.

There are several characteristics of situational leadership (*Situational Leadership and How Flexibility Leads to Success*, 2019). The most prominent characteristic is that a leader engaging in situational leadership gives directives based on follower readiness. A situational leadership style is a flexible approach to leadership as the leader attempts to understand the state of mind of the followers when giving directions. Situational leaders evaluate the maturity levels of the people in the organization and provide them the required support and direction. They require several important qualities to be successful including good communication, their ability to read their body language, the ability to understand the state of mind of the employees, and their ability to connect with the emotions of their team.

Situational leadership is associated with an increased awareness of the organizational situation (*Situational Leadership and How Flexibility Leads to Success*, 2019). Situational leadership can be helpful for change management within an organization as there is considerable uncertainty associated with the process of change. Some employees can take change positively while reacting to it in a negative manner. A leader can apply situational leadership skills including honesty and good communication to provide them with the information required to understand the vision and goals of an organization. Over time, leaders can use their situational leadership skills to increase the productivity and efficiency of an organization.

Leadership Flexibility in the Post-COVID Era

The post-COVID era requires an unconventional and flexible style of working, by being honest and transparent with yourself and the people you work with. High-profile employees often find it challenging to strike a work-life balance that allows them to spend time with their families while also fulfilling work commitments (*Our North American leader talks work flexibility amid COVID-19*, 2020). Establishing the right balance requires careful planning, taking vacations and leaves to spend time with the family, while also having enough time to be available to clients and stakeholders when they need your services.

There are several major changes in the work environment due to the effects of the COVID crisis (*Our North American leader talks work flexibility amid COVID-19*, 2020):

- Travel has decreased a great deal, and while it gives leaders more time to focus on overlooked areas, there is far less clarity on the distinction between personal time and professional commitments.
- The newly worked out schedule often gives time to spend on tasks that rejuvenate you, including having more time for

- family, going for morning walks or cycling, and also getting enough sleep.
- Most people admit feeling more connected to their colleagues due to the time they spend virtually with their colleagues and clients. Working from home allows you to blur the boundaries between home and work, and you are able to understand your colleagues at a personal level.
- Families are able to come together during this time as they choose to cook and spend time together, celebrate holidays, and establish deeper bonds.
- Employees have begun to view their leaders from a new perspective as they expect to be guided and supported by them. Effective leadership in this era is all about building the emotional and mental resilience of employees by being compassionate and understanding.

Leaders must understand the need for flexibility in the post-COVID era for their employees and spearhead initiatives that allow them to define new constraints where their employees can strike a balance between their personal and professional lives. This is the essence of compassionate leadership, and it helps improve performance and gain more loyalty from stakeholders (*Our North American leader talks work flexibility amid COVID-19*, 2020). To be able to meet the needs of employees, leaders must engage in continuous feedback from their team, so they can roll out customized programs for employees.

To sum it all up, transparency, empathy, and flexibility are important aspects of survival in this high-stress era. Increased stress is related to difficult decision-making as employee concerns must be addressed promptly. Most employees have to deal with multiple responsibilities in their home such as caring for a child or a parent, and the best way to deal with the situation is to focus on the outcome and not the process. Separating tasks by their priority is an effective strategy, and providing essential information to employees makes them feel they are in control. Another way to empower employees is by allowing them to work on the projects that they think add value (Panetta, 2020). Finally, enlighten about expectations when they change, and address concerns about their goals and performance. Highlight the importance of self-care to your employees and encourage them to expend time and effort in caring for themselves and their families.

Chapter Summary

- Patience allows leaders to make a fair assessment of the situation and succeed in their purpose. Impatience is associated with financial problems.
- Patience helps leaders gain respect, improve productivity and progress, fosters a positive attitude, helps make good decisions, improves time management, and helps adapt to change.
- Self-awareness, kindness, positivity, and self-reflection help improve patience.
- Flexibility is a quality of strong leadership and encourages cooperation among team members, and spurs innovation and productivity.
- Leaders who implement flexibility may take on different styles including the adapter, macromanager, micromanager, coach, idol, revolutionary leader, trailblazer, or beloved leader.
- Situational leadership is the way to engage employees and promote productivity within the organization.
- The post-COVID period requires flexibility due to decreased travel, changed schedules, better family bonds, and many more unconventional situations.
- Leaders can succeed by defining new constraints and allowing employees to have a balance between their personal and professional lives.
- High stress levels during this period require leaders to show empathy, transparency, and flexibility.

Chapter Nine: Filling Your Self-Development Bucket

It's David's last day at the company. His little talk at the farewell get-together is as transformational as his presence in the company for the past forty years. He has unexpected counsel for his team. They can never appreciate David enough for his contribution as a leader and listen intently to what he says. As he addresses his team, something terrific unfolds that will stay with them for the rest of their lives. David leaves no stone unturned in being an intentional leader …

Self-Development is about Inculcating Ethics and Integrity, and Requires Persistence

Self-Development Requires an Understanding of Areas to Improve and Strategies to Achieve Goals

"Adieu David, but we will Grow!"

David is the beloved leader, and most respected not just for his seniority, but for all the good things he did for his team. He made a real difference by supporting his team members sometimes, and going an extra mile for the company at other times. Today is David's farewell get together. This was his last year with the company and David still feels he needs to convey something to the team.

What could it possibly be?

David: Team, it's my last day with you in this company. This has been my second home for the past forty years, and I cannot thank you all enough for your great companionship. I feel like a mentor today, and I want to say something to you, which if you follow, will make a difference to you and the ones around you.

[The team listens eagerly]

David: I am going to stress the importance of self-development. To be a good team member and an asset to the company, you must not stop growing. You need to develop in a number of respects such as the spiritual, mental, and physical spheres. You need to develop good relationship skills and be generous to be a great person. I have seen life, and I cannot stress this enough, that integrity and ethics is more important than anything else for the company... and for you! So I want you to start planning now, and make a good plan for your future growth. Discipline yourself, understand your strengths, and consult a coach if you have to, but make sure you practice self-development.

[Team nods in agreement]

David: Become a self-leader with the right mindset and goals. Make a plan to improve your performance over say, six months, and settle for it with a winning attitude and an approach that works. Above all, communicate well and take ownership of your decisions. I will not be there after today, but I want you to never stop growing!

Team: [In unison]: Adieu David, but we will Grow!

Growing as a leader involves quantitative as well as qualitative development of skills and developing a good understanding of leadership. It is a continuous process and eventually has a lasting impact on the entire organization. It leads to the development of two extremely important traits that define the success of organizations - integrity and ethics. Personal development demands a lot of self-discipline and persistence (Cheprasov, 2021). One must possess the desire to learn, understand motivations, and ask the right questions. Moreover, regular interactions with peers, managers, and direct reports. are all essential and require good communication for successful personal development.

Importance of Personal Development

Success is seldom the result of college education, skills, or money. It is the result of an effort that most people put in to become a better person in life. Personal development is an extremely important aspect of life and affects not just your career success and growth, but also your personal and professional relationships (Creaswood, 2020). Personal development helps you grow, evolve, and mature, and reflects in several spheres of life as explained below:

- Spiritual Development: Developing spiritually is an essential aspect of personal development. Spiritual development helps not only those people who believe in God but also those that do not. All people can grow spiritually and find inner peace, which helps them focus, get over conflict, and deal with stress effectively.
- Relationship Skills: Getting along with people and understanding them helps to inculcate empathy and leads to successful relationships. People who are successful with their relationships know how and when to assert themselves, and they are intuitive and also care about others. They have

the ability to handle conflict effectively and are able to develop their relationships, continually, to reach new levels. People with good relationship skills are able to understand their specific deficits such as whether they are being too impatient or if they tend to avoid conflict.

- <u>Educating Yourself</u>: Most people think that it is only necessary to acquire the education that is needed to do their job well. However, education is beyond the skills required to complete your job and related to that which makes a person a good citizen. Staying on top of the news to learn about current events, undertaking online courses on a variety of topics, and visiting libraries, community centers, and museums to enrich your skills and knowledge, all count towards educating oneself.
- <u>Practicing Generosity</u>: There's more to generosity than what most people perceive i.e. giving charity or donations. While these acts express generosity, they do ot account for the real meaning attached to generosity. Being generous means making the well-being of other people a high priority, knowing them well to understand their needs, and trying your best to fulfill those needs. This practice is all about being generous in relationships and adds value to your contribution as well as those around you.
- <u>Developing your Physical and Mental Health</u>: Most people overlook mental and physical development although they are extremely essential for personal development. The impact of physical health reflects on your focus, energy levels, mood, and concentration. Physical development is essential for socialization and active participation with family and friends. Furthermore, mental health, when ignored, can sabotage your relationships and result in burnout. Further to meeting the need to cater to your appointments, maintaining your physical and mental health is a restorative activity that

involves regular exercise, sleep, and pursuing the activities that recharge you.

Most people underestimate the value of self-development and spend their life doing the same mundane jobs day after day, underestimating their potential and never setting goals for personal growth. They generally see no significant improvements in their mental, emotional, or physical health, and having no desires or dreams leaves them without fulfillment (Homer, 2020). Self-development helps you to plan your life and have confidence in what you are doing as well as a certain degree of certainty for better outcomes in your career, relationships, and finances. This approach helps us build a strong mindset and overcome negative emotions. A positive mindset is essential as it prevents you from leading a mediocre life, always dissatisfied with what you have and looking for others to push the blame for what happened.

Key Areas For Improvement With Personal Development

Personal development can be the means to improve essential leadership qualities (*Continuously Improve as a Leader*, n.d.):

- Improve your listening skills to gain a better understanding of how the team works, by understanding what people say, their body language, and mood.
- Inculcate your capability to manage and resolve conflict, and develop the traits that lead to it, including the ability to be politically correct at certain times, analyze objectively, and listen empathetically.
- Develop objectivism to account for facts and emotions, and weigh them for a successful analysis. This quality helps evaluate past decisions to avoid committing the same mistakes in the future.

- Spend time to update your <u>technical skills</u> by understanding which skill will be important for your role and how it contributes towards organizational development

Strategies for Successful Self-Development

Experts indicate that effective leadership and followership are the results of developing key traits in leaders including stress resistance, decision-making, and good listening skills. These strengths in leaders are extremely essential and make followers overlook other weaknesses (Richard, 2016; Moore, 2019). Effective leadership is the result of being self-aware, authentic, and having good character and integrity. To display essential skills and traits, and have good followership, leaders must invest in their self-development. By engaging in self-development through immersion learning and experiential learning, leaders can increase their effectiveness. Here are a few strategies leaders can follow towards their self-development:

- Measure your leadership qualities and style by taking tests and understand your strengths and traits.
- Rather than always looking at ways to fix performance problems, develop the areas where you have the ability to do exceptionally well.
- Focus on one goal at a time to bring about a measurable improvement in your strengths. This is better than working on a long list of areas of improvement.
- Take help from an executive coach to figure out the best way to develop your strengths.
- Set specific goals you can measure and achieve, and have a third party evaluate your behavior and assess if you have reached a specific milestone.
- Inculcate self-discipline to achieve personal and organizational goals.

- Ensure you have the right balance between personal life and work and maintain a compassionate outlook to gain respect from your team.
- Connect goals to outcomes that matter to you to make it easy to attain them.
- Get feedback on your progress and measure your performance frequently by engaging a reliable source to be consistent with your success
- Learning is a continuous process, and aiming high helps you become an effective leader, innovate, and utilize new opportunities.

Zigarmi (2018) introduces the concept of self-leadership, which is the leadership undertaken by an individual, intentionally, to steer themselves and their team towards a common goal. It helps you manage your energy to initiate and perform at a high level while keeping your team motivated. Self-leadership is an empowering and inspiring activity. In doing so, you align your goals with that of the organization and achieve success through the empowerment of the employees. Self-leadership can be implemented through several strategies including goal setting, aligning goals with team priorities, tracking daily progress, time management, and maintaining a schedule.

Strategies to Implement Self-Leadership to Manage Organizational Goals

Self-leadership is an important aspect of success even when you are not in a formal leadership role. Even when you are a member of the team, self-leadership helps to set a strategy to achieve the goal without counting on the manager or a coworker to change things. Given the fact that self-leadership moves beyond simply taking initiative and deciding on the best course of action. There are several ways to implement self-leadership (Zigarmi, 2018). You can pursue your goals in the way you think is appropriate or pursue them using a strategy that is also implemented by the organization. Alternatively, you can also develop a strategy that is useful to you as well as the organization. The best ways to manage organizational goals and encourage growth are summarized below:

- Clarity on Goals: It is important to have clarity about your values as your leadership style is reflected in your interpersonal relationships with colleagues. Your mission and goals must be aligned and your employees must be encouraged to follow through.
- Constant Mindset: Take time to recenter and evaluate your mindset to have constant focus and flexibility when meeting organizational goals. Having a constant positive mindset ensures that when goals and plans undergo change, you are still in the position to meet the needs of the organization.
- Performance Plan: Your role in the organization determines the goals you set, and your daily activities culminate to meet those goals. Planning is very important to achieve high performance standards. Planning enables you to intentionally make a difference in the way you carry out your day-to-day activities. While planning, make a schedule and allot time for your leadership tasks and measure possible improvements.
- Consistent Approach: Effective leadership requires consistency. All members of the team must understand and follow information about leadership competencies that managers set up in an organization. Understanding and applying these competencies ensures that performance is evaluated consistently and teams are able to effectively collaborate throughout the organization.
- Proactive Attitude: Having a clear role, goals, and plan is effective only when you are able to react to the situation when a problem occurs. Challenges can be dealt with by

applying self-leadership skills to be able to progress towards the goal and solve problems.

Essential Character Traits for Successful Personal Development

Our leadership skills are primarily based on our life experiences The situations we come across in life provide clarity and adversities influence our thinking. Eventually, we see significant changes in our leadership approach. Personal development is all about having confidence, self-awareness, goals, and the ability to deal with challenges in an honest manner (Montillo, 2015). Personal development requires you to inculcate important character traits:

- Asking Questions: Asking questions out of curiosity is an essential part of intellectual development. Good research skills and the ability to develop your knowledge, as well as getting feedback from mentors and colleagues are part of developing as a successful leader. Curiosity must lead you to explore and understand existing processes for possible enhancements and improvements that contribute to the overall optimization of operations.
- Being Ethical: Effective leaders believe in doing the right thing for the advantage of stakeholders, employees, and the community. Integrity is an essential aspect of successful leadership and those who are engaged in dishonesty and cutting corners cannot contribute any value to the organization. Focusing on integrity and ethics nurtures positivity about yourself and the people you work with.
- Communicating Well: Effective communication is an essential aspect of productivity. Communication in a fast-paced world gives you only a few minutes to communicate your stance. To be effective, you have to perform your research, answer questions, and put your point in a concise

manner. Effective leaders develop their speaking and writing skills to be able to present their ideas convincingly.
- Working in a Team: Project success in an organization is the result of contribution from the whole team. To be able to work in a team, it is important to understand your role and the roles of your team members. To gain a well-rounded understanding of how the organization works, it is important to not just understand the operations within your department, but also how things work in other departments. To make a significant contribution, it is important to maintain good interpersonal relationships. It is a good idea to keep aside some time to know about the different employees in different departments, from the front-line staff to the senior executives. This practice helps you build and maintain good rapport with the team and contributes to the overall success of the company
- Taking Ownership: Taking ownership of work, and admitting not just your successes but also your mistakes, leads to productivity. When you acknowledge that you are responsible for the outcome of your work and department, you are more likely to realize improvements and result-based outcomes.

Chapter Summary

- Quantitative and qualitative self-development skills are important for good leadership and foster ethical values and integrity.
- Personal development requires excelling in several areas including spiritual skills, physical and mental health, being generous, getting education, and developing relationship skills.
- Personal development can help you improve in a number of areas including objectivism, technical skills, conflict resolution, and listening skills.
- Self-development can be a strategic process that incorporates self-discipline, feedback, measurable and achievable goals, and many more aspects.
- Self-leadership is an important way to achieve success without expecting a colleague or manager to change things for you.
- Self-leadership can be implemented by having clear goals, a performance plan, a constant mindset, a proactive attitude, and a consistent approach.
- Successful personal development can be achieved through important character traits such as being ethical, communicating effectively, working in a team, asking questions, and taking ownership.

Conclusion

Intentional leadership is a path-breaking strategy that can enable you to bring about transformational change within your team and your organization. This book teaches you exactly how to do it. "The Power of Intentional Leadership" covers every little detail you need to know to become a fully capable intentional leader.

Guided by a simple case study of David and Goliath, it absorbs your attention from the start to the end, teaching you how to inculcate the absolutely important character traits from the ground up. If you want to be a leader that is remembered by the team, then this is a must-read and a definite way to your leadership success.

References

Ackerman, C. E. (2019, July 4). Positive Leadership: 30 Must-Have Traits and Skills. PositivePsychology.com. https://positivepsychology.com/positive-leadership/

Albritton, K. (2015, January 26). The Characteristics of the "Intentional Leader." PRNEWS. https://www.prnewsonline.com/the-characteristics-of-the-intentional-leader/

Avolio, B. J., & Gardner, W. L. (2005). Authentic leadership development: Getting to the root of positive forms of leadership. The Leadership Quarterly, 16(3), 315–338. https://doi.org/10.1016/j.leaqua.2005.03.001

Balance, F. B. F. T. F. J. R. wrote about business management for T., & Reh, has 30 years of experience as a business manager R. T. B. editorial policies F. J. (2020, January 17). Here's the Positive Trait That Makes a Great Leader and Manager. The Balance Careers. https://www.thebalancecareers.com/leaders-are-always-positive-2275805

Bass, B. M., & Riggio, R. E. (2006). Transformational leadership (2nd ed.). Routledge.

Byrd, D. (2020). 5 Essential Mindsets for High-Performing Teams. Experienced to Lead. https://www.experiencetolead.com/5-essential-mindsets-for-high-performing-teams/

Cameron, K. S. (2008). Positive leadership. San Francisco, CA: Berrett-Koehler Publishers, Inc.

Clark, L. (2020, February 19). Mind over matter: leadership mindsets and actions to drive results. Chief Learning Officer - CLO

Media. https://www.chieflearningofficer.com/2020/02/19/mind-over-matter-leadership-mindsets-and-actions-to-drive-results/

Gottfredson, R., & Reina, C. (2020, January 17). To Be a Great Leader, You Need the Right Mindset. Harvard Business Review. https://hbr.org/2020/01/to-be-a-great-leader-you-need-the-right-mindset

Gottfredson, R. (2018, May 12). The Key to Effective Leadership: Mindsets | Leading Blog: A Leadership Blog. Www.leadershipnow.com. https://www.leadershipnow.com/leadingblog/2018/12/the_key_to_effective_leadershi.html

Hogan, C. (2016, August 15). 9 Tips to Become an Intentional Leader. SUCCESS. https://www.success.com/9-tips-to-become-an-intentional-leader/

Reh, J. (2020). Here's the Positive Trait That Makes a Great Leader and Manager. The Balance Careers. https://www.thebalancecareers.com/leaders-are-always-positive-2275805

Richards, T. (2012, June 19). All Leaders Must Cast Vision. Clearvision. https://www.clearvisiondevelopment.com/post/all-leaders-must-cast-vision

Youssef, C. M., & Luthans, F. (2012). Positive global leadership. Journal of World Business, 47(4), 539–547. https://doi.org/10.1016/j.jwb.2012.01.007

Chapiewski, G. (2020, May 11). What is the "Say vs. Do" ratio about and why does it matter more than you think. Medium. https://gc.zone/what-is-the-say-vs-do-ratio-about-and-why-does-it-matter-more-than-you-think-308d18ce600

Debevoise, N. D. (2020, November 5). Make Accountability Matter Again: Increase Your Say:Do Ratio To Build Trust. Forbes. https://www.forbes.com/sites/nelldebevoise/2020/11/05/make-accountability-matter-again-increase-your-saydo-ratio-to-build-trust/?sh=1826728a7dab

Deeb, G. (2019). Leadership 101: Narrow Your Say-Do Gap. Forbes. https://www.forbes.com/sites/georgedeeb/2019/05/02/leadership-101-narrow-your-say-do-gap/?sh=17d0e0392420

Peterson, J. (2020, February 4). Building Trust By Closing The "Say-Do" Gap. ChiefExecutive.net. https://chiefexecutive.net/building-trust-by-closing-the-say-do-gap/#:~:text=The%20first%20law%20of%20trust

Sluss, D. (2020, April 16). Stepping into a Leadership Role? Be Ready to Tell Your Story. Harvard Business Review. https://hbr.org/2020/04/stepping-into-a-leadership-role-be-ready-to-tell-your-story

Branham, L. (n.d.). The 7 Hidden Reasons Employees Leave. https://leadershipbeyondlimits.com/wp-content/uploads/2013/06/WhyPeopleLeave-Branham.pdf

Dowden, C. (2013). *Forget ethics training: Focus on empathy*. Financial Post. https://financialpost.com/executive/c-suite/forget-ethics-training-focus-on-empathy

Eikenberry, K. (2019). *Creating a Communication Cadence*. Kevin Eikenberry on Leadership & Learning. https://blog.kevineikenberry.com/personal-professional-development/creating-communication-cadence/

Ferry, K. (2016). Korn Ferry Hay Group Research Proves Employee Engagement Drops During Organizational Change. Www.businesswire.com.

https://www.businesswire.com/news/home/20161010005181/en/Korn-Ferry-Hay-Group-Research-Proves-Employee-Engagement-Drops-During-Organizational-Change

Gentle, S. (2017). The State of Miscommunication: New Survey Finds Communication Gaps Across Organizations | Onrec. Www.onrec.com. https://www.onrec.com/news/news-archive/the-state-of-miscommunication-new-survey-finds-communication-gaps-across#:~:text=More%20than%2080%20percent%20of

Goman, C. K. (2018). 5 Ways Body Language Impacts Leadership Results. Forbes. https://www.forbes.com/sites/carolkinseygoman/2018/08/26/5-ways-body-language-impacts-leadership-results/

Jensen, S. (2019). Poor Internal Communication Can Be a Costly Mistake for Businesses. Workforce.com. https://www.workforce.com/news/poor-internal-communication-can-be-a-costly-mistake-for-businesses

Jouany, V., & Martic, K. (2021). 18 Leadership Communication Trends to Look For in 2021. Blog.smarp.com. https://blog.smarp.com/18-leadership-communication-trends-to-look-for-in-2020

Kenexa Research Institute announces world rankings for employee engagement. (2009). Personnel Today. https://www.personneltoday.com/hr/kenexa-research-institute-announces-world-rankings-for-employee-engagement/#:~:text=The%20research%20examines%20the%20impact

Landry, L. (2019). Communication Skills Every Leader Needs. Business Insights - Blog. https://online.hbs.edu/blog/post/leadership-communication

Leadership & Cadence: Communication -- More than Just Words. (n.d.). EMS World. https://www.emsworld.com/article/10323462/leadership-cadence-communication-more-just-words

Leonard, C. (2020). *Effective Leadership Communication Priorities During COVID-19.* Www.snapcomms.com. https://www.snapcomms.com/blog/effective-leadership-communication-covid19

Myatt, M. (2012). *10 Communication Secrets Of Great Leaders.* Forbes. https://www.forbes.com/sites/mikemyatt/2012/04/04/10-communication-secrets-of-great-leaders/?sh=3d6cb72022fe

Napolitano, A. (2016). Beyond the Clock: The Benefits of Highly Motivated Employees. Business.com; business.com. https://www.business.com/articles/the-benefits-of-highly-motivated-employees/

Parmar, B. (2016). The Most Empathetic Companies, 2016. Harvard Business Review. https://hbr.org/2016/12/the-most-and-least-empathetic-companies-2016

Project.co. (2020). Communication Statistics 2020 (New Data). Project.co. https://www.project.co/communication-statistics-2020/#:~:text=65%25%20of%20businesses%20primarily%20use

www.recruiter.com. (2013). Survey: Poor Communication Largest Factor in Morale Problems. Recruiter. https://www.recruiter.com/i/survey-poor-communication-largest-factor-in-morale-problems/

Wishart, J. (2019). *5 Reasons Why You Need The Right KPIs in 2020 (Infographic).* Rhythmsystems.com. https://www.rhythmsystems.com/blog/5-reasons-why-you-need-kpis-infographic

Write, H. (n.d.). *Leadership Communication Skills: The Complete Guide*. Www.hurleywrite.com. https://www.hurleywrite.com/Blog/92445/Leadership-Communication-Skills-The-Complete-Guide

Austin, J. B. (2016). *Master the One-on-One Meeting*. HBS Working Knowledge. https://hbswk.hbs.edu/item/master-the-one-on-one-meeting

Bad Company Culture Definition and Its Impact. (2019). LSA Global. https://lsaglobal.com/blog/how-a-bad-company-culture-impacts-business-results/

Hassell, D. (2017). *The Only One On One Meeting Checklist You Will Ever Need*. 15Five. https://www.15five.com/blog/one-on-one-meeting-checklist/

"How Much?" Here's Why You Should Invest in Feedback Culture. (n.d.). Www.leapsome.com. https://www.leapsome.com/blog/the-roi-on-feedback-culture-time-to-supercharge-your-employee-engagement

Sull, D. S. and C. (2020). *How Companies Are Winning on Culture During COVID-19*. MIT Sloan Management Review. https://sloanreview.mit.edu/article/how-companies-are-winning-on-culture-during-covid-19/

Stewart, N. (n.d.). *7 Tips on How to Conduct a Meaningful Personal Development Review*. Newman Stewart. https://newmanstewart.co.uk/news/2018/04/7-tips-on-how-to-conduct-a-meaningful-personal-development-review/90

Why does your company need a strong feedback culture? (n.d.). Impraise. https://www.impraise.com/blog/why-does-your-company-need-a-strong-feedback-culture

Cranwell, R. (2018). The Praise-Criticism Ratio You Should Be Using With Your Agents. Stella Connect. https://stellaconnect.com/blog/the-praise-criticism-ratio-you-should-be-using-with-your-agents/

Finkelstein, S. R., & Fishbach, A. (2012). Tell Me What I Did Wrong: Experts Seek and Respond to Negative Feedback. *Journal of Consumer Research*, *39*(1), 22–38. https://doi.org/10.1086/661934

Iarocci, J. (2018). Servant-Leaders Praise More, Criticize Less. Cairnway Coaching. https://serveleadnow.com/servant-leaders-praise-more-criticize-less/

Pandey, M. (2019). 3 Key Lessons We Can Learn From the One Minute Manager. Dumb Little Man. https://www.dumblittleman.com/3-key-lessons-we-can-learn-from-one/

North, T. (2019). What's the Right Balance of Praise and Criticism? ColoradoBiz Magazine. https://www.cobizmag.com/whats-the-right-balance-of-praise-and-criticism/

Scott, K. (n.d.-a). Praise In Public, Criticize In Private. Www.radicalcandor.com. Retrieved March 9, 2021, from https://www.radicalcandor.com/public-praise-private-criticism/

Scott, K. (n.d.-b). *A HIP Approach To Feedback*. Www.radicalcandor.com. https://www.radicalcandor.com/a-hip-approach-to-feedback/

Tanner, R. (2020). Praise in Public, Correct in Private. Management Is a Journey®. https://managementisajourney.com/in-100-words-public-humiliation-is-a-flawed-motivation-strategy/

Blue Beyond Consulting. (2020). *Leading Through Uncertainty: Lessons in Change Leadership*. Blue Beyond Consulting. https://www.bluebeyondconsulting.com/2020/04/leading-through-uncertainty-lessons-in-change-leadership/

Bruce, J. (2020). *Change Fatigue Is Threatening Your Business*. Talent Management & HR. https://www.tlnt.com/change-fatigue-is-threatening-your-business/

Gaskell, C. (2019). *The new rules to leading people through change*. Training Zone. https://www.trainingzone.co.uk/lead/culture/the-new-rules-to-leading-people-through-change

Greenberg, S. (2020). *10 Ways to Support Your Team in the COVID-19 Crisis*. Talent Management and HR. https://www.tlnt.com/10-ways-to-support-your-team-in-the-covid-19-crisis/

Ratanjee, V., & Gandhi, V. (2020). *3 Strategies for Leading Effectively Amid COVID-19*. Gallup.com; Gallup. https://www.gallup.com/workplace/306503/strategies%20leading%20effectively%20amid%20covid.aspx

Ruhmann, J. (2020). *Leading through Change in 2021*. Level up Leadership. https://levelupleadership.com/leading-through-change-in-2021/

Sturt, D., & Nordstrom, T. (2016). *6 Dos And Don'ts Of Leading Through Change*. Forbes. https://www.forbes.com/sites/davidsturt/2016/05/13/6-dos-and-donts-of-leading-through-change/

Wolf, J. (2020). *11 Ways Leaders Can Lead Through the COVID-19 Pandemic*. Talent Management HR.

https://www.tlnt.com/11-ways-leaders-can-lead-through-the-covid-19-pandemic/

Wood, A. (2019). *Leadership Communication During Times Of Change*. Forbes. https://www.forbes.com/sites/forbescoachescouncil/2019/04/25/leadership-communication-during-times-of-change-10-ways-to-move-forward-together/

Cheprasov, A. (2021). *Personal Growth as a Leader*. Study.com. https://study.com/academy/lesson/personal-growth-as-a-leader.html

Continuously Improve as a Leader. (n.d.). Www.skillsyouneed.com. https://www.skillsyouneed.com/rhubarb/continuously-improve-leadership.html

Creaswood, K. (2020). *Personal Development as a Critical Factor to Success*. The Personal Development Magazine. https://peopledevelopmentmagazine.com/2020/02/09/personal-development-journey/

Homer, M. (2020). *Why Self-Development is Important if You Want to Be a True Leader*. Business 2 Community. https://www.business2community.com/leadership/why-self-development-is-important-if-you-want-to-be-a-true-leader-02282427

Montillo, A. (2015). *Effective Leadership is About Personal Growth*. Cameron School of Business Blog. https://blogs.stthom.edu/cameron/effective-leadership-is-about-personal-growth/

Moore, J. (2019). *What Every Leader Needs to Know About Personal Development*. Everyday Power.

https://everydaypower.com/every-leader-needs-know-personal-development/

Richard, L. (2016). *Toward Better Leadership: Self-Development, Strengths & Flaws*. Legal Executive Institute. https://www.legalexecutiveinstitute.com/toward-better-leadership/#

Zigarmi, D. (2018). *The Importance of Self-Leadership and How to Leverage It to Improve Organizational Leadership*. Medium. https://medium.com/@dzigarmi/the-importance-of-self-leadership-and-how-to-leverage-it-to-improve-organizational-leadership-f32ffb64938c

Haggerty, M. (2020). *Flexibility Makes You a Stronger Leader. Here's How to Practice It*. Inc.com. https://www.inc.com/maria-haggerty/flexibility-makes-you-a-stronger-leader-heres-how-to-practice-it.html

Harmon, J. (2014). *The Power of a Patient Leader*. Brilliance within Coaching. https://brilliancewithincoaching.com/servant%20leadership/the-power-of-a-patient-leader

Moran. (2010). *Leading with Patience – The Will to Wait*. If You Will Lead - Enduring Wisdom for Those Who Choose to Lead. https://ifyouwilllead.com/leading-with-patience-the-will-to-wait

OKeefe, M. (2014). *How to be a Flexible Leader: 8 Styles for Different Situations*. Lifehack. https://www.lifehack.org/articles/productivity/how-flexible-leader-8-styles-for-different-situations.html

Our North American leader talks work flexibility amid COVID-19. (2020). www.mckinsey.com. https://www.mckinsey.com/about-us/new-at-mckinsey-blog/our-north-american-managing-partner-talks-work-flexibility-in-a-post-covid-world

Panetta, K. (2020). *Manage Employee Stress With Flexibility and Transparency*. www.gartner.com. https://www.gartner.com/smarterwithgartner/manage-employee-stress-with-flexibility-and-transparency/

Patience and Leadership in Our Current World. (2021). Leadership Delta. https://www.leadershipdelta.com/be-the-delta-blog/2021/2/10/patience-and-leadership-in-our-current-world

Situational Leadership and How Flexibility Leads to Success. (2019). The Enterprise World. https://www.theenterpriseworld.com/situational

Todorovic, J. (2019). *12 Reasons Why Having Patience in Leadership is Important*. RLX Business Solutions. https://relax.ph/blog/patience-in-leadership/

Fiore, M. (2016). *Upping your game as a leader? Consider the duck!* www.linkedin.com. https://www.linkedin.com/pulse/upping-your-game-leader-consider-duck-martin-fiore/

McBride, L. (2015). *Duck-inspired lessons in leadership*. The Independent. https://theindependent.ca/2015/12/05/duck-inspired-lessons-in-leadership/

Palizban, A. (2012). *7 Lessons We Can Learn From Geese to Succeed at Work*. OKRs and Performance Management. https://7geese.com/7-lessons-we-can-learn-from-geese-to-succeed-at-work/

Poke, D. (2011). *4 Important Leadership Lessons From Ducks*. Better Life Coaching Blog. https://betterlifecoachingblog.com/2011/12/08/4-important-leadership-lessons-from-ducks/

Rosenberg, A. (2012). *Lead like a duck*. Leadership Louisville Center. https://www.leadershiplouisville.org/lead-like-a-duck/

www.ingramcontent.com/pod-product-compliance
Lightning Source LLC
Chambersburg PA
CBHW070108230526
45472CB00004B/1166